HOUSING ACT 1988

A Practical Guide to Private Residential Lettings

WILDE SAPTE

Graham Bennett LLB, *Partner, Wilde Sapte*
Robert Lee LLB, *Director of Education,*
Wilde Sapte

BSP PROFESSIONAL BOOKS
OXFORD LONDON EDINBURGH
BOSTON MELBOURNE

First published 1989

British Library
Cataloguing in Publication Data
Bennett, Graham
  Housing Act 1988: a practical guide
  to private residential lettings.
  1. Great Britain. Housing. Law:
  Housing Act 1988
  I. Title   II. Lee, Robert
  III. Wilde Sapte
  344.104′63535

  ISBN 0-632-02627-8

BSP Professional Books
A division of Blackwell Scientific
  Publications Ltd
Editorial Offices:
Osney Mead, Oxford OX2 0EL
  (Orders: Tel. 0865 240201)
8 John Street, London WC1N 2ES
23 Ainslie Place, Edinburgh EH3 6AJ
3 Cambridge Center, Suite 208, Cambridge
  MA 02142, USA
107 Barry Street, Carlton, Victoria 3053,
  Australia

Set by DP Photosetting, Aylesbury, Bucks
Printed and bound in Great Britain by
Mackays of Chatham PLC, Chatham, Kent

Pages 2–21 of Statutory Instrument 1988 No 2203, which appear in Appendix III, are reproduced
with the permission of the Controller of Her Majesty's Stationery Office.

Contents

Preface

This book aims to take a 'no nonsense' look at the cornerstones of the Housing Act 1988 which may directly affect most practitioners, institutions, developers and funders. We therefore deal with assured and assured shorthold tenancies, transitional provisions, protection from eviction, the new role of rent assessment committees and rent officers, the Business Expansion Scheme and certain general provisions of the Act including premiums on long leases, repairing obligations in short leases and amendments made by the Housing Act 1988 to the Landlord and Tenant Act 1987. In order specifically to assist the practitioner the subjects covered have been dealt with so far as possible in the order in which they are dealt with under the Housing Act 1988. The law is stated as at 26 April 1989.

The provisions of Part I of the Housing Act 1988, which form the subject of this work, do not extend to Scotland. However, given the similar nature of the provisions of Part II of the Housing (Scotland) Act 1988, the book is written in the hope that it will serve some use for fellow-practitioners north of the border.

There are many people who helped in the production of this book. Our thanks go to everyone who assisted and in particular to Richard Barham without whom this book would probably never have been written.

Graham Bennett and Bob Lee   26 April 1989
Wilde Sapte
Queensbridge House
60 Upper Thames Street
London EC4V 3BD

Abbreviations of Statutes

AA 1967	Agriculture Act 1967
AHA 1986	Agricultural Holdings Act 1986
CA 1960	Charities Act 1960
CCA 1984	County Courts Act 1984
CLA 1977	Criminal Law Act 1977
DVMPA 1976	Domestic Violence and Matrimonial Proceedings Act 1976
FA 1983	Finance Act 1983
FA 1988	Finance Act 1988
GRA 1967	General Rate Act 1967
HA 1957	Housing Act 1957
HA 1980	Housing Act 1980
HA 1985	Housing Act 1985
HAA 1985	Housing Associations Act 1985
HFA 1972	Housing Finance Act 1972
HPA	Housing and Planning Act 1986
HSA 1988	Housing (Scotland) Act 1988
IA 1986	Insolvency Act 1986
ICTA 1988	Income and Corporation Taxes Act 1988
LGA 1972	Local Government Act 1972
LPA 1925	Law of Property Act 1925
LPA 1969	Law of Property Act 1969
LTA 1927	Landlord and Tenant Act 1927
LTA 1954	Landlord and Tenant Act 1954
LTA 1985	Landlord and Tenant Act 1985
LTA 1987	Landlord and Tenant Act 1987
LTA 1988	Landlord and Tenant Act 1988
MHA 1983	Matrimonial Homes Act 1983
PFEA 1977	Protection from Eviction Act 1977
RA 1968	Rent Act 1968
RA 1977	Rent Act 1977
RAA 1976	Rent (Agriculture) Act 1976
SSA 1986	Social Security Act 1986
TIA 1971	Tribunals and Inquiries Act 1971

Chapter 1

Introduction

One of the aims of the Housing Act 1988 (now referred to throughout this book simply as the 'Act') is to halt the decline in private rented housing.

To this end the Act introduces the 'assured tenancy' and the 'assured shorthold tenancy' – for both of which rent controls and security of tenure are reduced in comparison to the protection enjoyed by tenancies falling within the protection of the Rent Act 1977 ('RA 1977'). It is not possible to contract out of the Act. The Act, however, has no retrospective application. Part I only affects tenancies granted after 15 January 1989. The RA 1977 continues to apply to tenancies created under that Act before 15 January 1989.

The key features of these new forms of tenancies are as follows.

(1) Assured tenancy

The key features are:

(a) letting at market rents (with very limited statutory intervention)
(b) the grounds on which a court may order possession are more extensive than under RA 1977
(c) landlords no longer have to be 'approved' as required by assured tenancies under the Housing Act 1980 ('HA 1980').

(2) Assured shorthold tenancies

The key features are:

(a) initial letting at market rents (but subject to reference to a rent assessment committee)
(b) minimum term of six months
(c) landlord has an automatic right to a court order for possession.

How far is the Act in force?

In terms of the material covered in this text, the Act is in force. It may be necessary to know the commencement date for particular provisions. The following sections of the Act came into force on the following days:

15 November 1988 (by Royal Assent)	Part III (Housing Action Trusts) ss.132, 133, 134 ss.138, 139 s.141
1 December 1988 (SI 1988 No. 2056)	ss.46(1), 46(2) s.47(2) s.47(6) (in relation to s.47(2)) s.140(1) (in relation to Schedule 17 paras 91, 92, 93, 94, 95, 96, 98, 99, 100, 101, 102, 104, 105, 114, 115, 116)
2 January 1989 (SI 1988 No. 2152)	s.140(1) (in relation to Schedule 17 paras 77, 78, 85, 86, 87, 88, 90) s.140(2) (in relation to Schedule 18 repealing words in s.38 Housing (Scotland) Act 1988)
15 January 1989 (by s.141(3))	Part I (Rented Accommodation) ss.115, 116, 117, 118 ss.120, 121 s.123 ss.125, 126, 127 ss.130, 131 ss.136, 137
15 January 1989 (SI 1988 No. 2152)	s.49 s.57 s.59(1) ss.59(2) and (3) (in relation to Schedule 6 paras 1, 8(2), 25 and 26) s.94 s.106 ss.111, 112, 113, 114 s.119 (subject to transitional provisions) s.140(1) (in relation to Schedule 17 paras 1–16, 17(2), 18–37, 40, 42–65, 67–76, 80–84 and subject to transitional provisions) s.140(2) (in part and subject to transitional provisions)

10 March 1989   s.122
(SI 1989 No. 203)   s.124
                     s.140(1) (in relation to Schedule 17 para. 41)

1 April 1989   Part II (Housing Associations) (except s.59 in
(SI 1989 No. 404)   relation to para. 27 of Schedule 6)
                     s.129
                     s.140(1) (in relation to paragraphs 66, 89, 97,
                     103 and 106–13 of Schedule 17)
                     s.140(2) (in part)

5 April 1989   Part IV (all remaining provisions)
(SI 1989 No. 404)   s.127
                     s.140(1) (in relation to paragraphs 17(1), 38
                     and 39 of Schedule 17)

Chapter 2

Residential Tenancies prior to the Housing Act 1988

2.01 Introduction

Under the law as it stood prior to the Act, the following main forms of tenancies were regulated by statute:

(1) Protected tenancies and statutory tenancies (RA 1977)
(2) Housing association lettings and licences (RA 1977 and the Housing Act 1985 ('HA 1985'))
(3) Restricted contracts (RA 1977)
(4) Assured tenancies (HA 1980)
(5) Protected shorthold tenancies (HA 1980)

The effect of the Act on these is considered in detail in Chapter 5 (Transitional Provisions). In essence the Act provides (with limited exceptions) that none of these tenancies can be created after 15 January 1989.

The assured tenancy and assured shorthold tenancy introduced by the Act are *not* the same as the assured tenancy and shorthold tenancy created by HA 1980. This clash of nomenclature means that it is vital to distinguish the tenancies created under HA 1980 from those introduced by the Act. In essence HA 1980 freed certain tenancies that would otherwise have been protected tenancies or housing association tenancies from the security and rent controls of RA 1977. In order to appreciate this distinction we set out below a brief summary of the salient features of both an assured tenancy and a protected shorthold tenancy under HA 1980.

2.02 Assured tenancy: s.56 HA 1980

Briefly, to create an HA 1980 assured tenancy the landlord's interest must, since the creation of the tenancy, have belonged to a body approved by the Secretary of State. These bodies comprise developers, pension funds, insurance companies etc. such as Barratt Developments plc, Norwich Union Life Insurance Society and the Prudential Assurance Co. Ltd. In addition, one of two further requirements set out below must be satisfied:

(1) (a) The dwelling-house must be, or form part of, a building which was erected (and on which construction work first began) on or after 8 August 1980; and

    (b) prior to its occupation by the tenant, no part of it must have been occupied by any person as his residence except under an assured tenancy;

or

(2) (a) ground 1(a) above was extended by the Housing and Planning Act 1986 ('HPA 1986') to cover dwellings built prior to 8 August 1980 but which had been substantially improved, repaired or converted ('qualifying works') at a cost greater than a prescribed amount;

    (b) the dwelling-house must be fit for human habitation at the date of the grant of the first tenancy after completion of the qualifying works under which a person is entitled to occupy the dwelling-house as his residence; and

    (c) since the qualifying works no part of the dwelling-house must have been occupied by any person as his residence except under an assured tenancy, and the first residential letting after the conversion must not have been to someone who was entitled to occupy the dwelling-house as a protected or statutory tenant under RA 1977 or a protected occupier or statutory tenant under the Rent (Agriculture) Act 1976 ('RAA 1976') prior to the conversion.

Once an assured tenancy has been created (and subject to the tenancy being held by an approved body so that it remained 'assured'), it is governed by a regime that is similar to that set out in Part II of the Landlord and Tenant Act 1954 ('LTA 1954').

2.03   *Protected shorthold tenancy: ss.51–55 HA 1980*

Essentially a protected shorthold tenancy is a protected tenancy (within the meaning of the RA 1977) which is subject to a mandatory right of possession.

In addition to the tenancy qualifying as a protected tenancy within the meaning of RA 1977, the following conditions had to be satisfied:

(1) The term must have been granted after 28 November 1980 to a tenant who was not immediately beforehand a protected or statutory tenant within RA 1977 of those premises.

(2) The tenancy must (broadly) have been for a term certain of not less than one but not more than five years.

(3) The tenancy must have been granted on terms which did not allow the landlord to bring it to an end before the expiry of the term (otherwise than in pursuance of a proviso for re-entry or forfeiture for non-payment of rent or breach of any other obligation of the tenancy).

(4) Before the grant of the tenancy the landlord must have served a valid formal notice on the tenant that the tenancy was to be a protected shorthold tenancy; and

(5) As originally drawn HA 1980 required that the rent be registered when the tenancy was granted. If not, an application for registration must have been made within 28 days of the grant and, until the rent was registered, the rent charged had to be limited to the amount specified in a certificate of fair rent. As amended this condition only applies if:

    (a) the tenancy was granted on or after 28 November 1980 but before 1 December 1981 (wherever the dwelling-house stood); or

    (b) the tenancy was in Greater London and was granted on or after 1 December 1981 but before 4 May 1987.

Once created, the protected shorthold tenancy has two special characteristics. The first is that it is not capable of being assigned otherwise than in pursuance of a property adjustment order made in matrimonial proceedings. The second is that (in general) a sub-tenant of a protected shorthold tenant enjoys no security of tenure against the landlord of that protected shorthold tenant. Thus (from the landlord's point of view) possession against the tenant confers possession against the sub-tenant.

A landlord cannot determine a protected shorthold tenancy prematurely. A tenant, however, has this right upon giving one month's notice if the term certain is two years or less, and three months' notice if the term exceeds this period.

The primary feature of a protected shorthold tenancy from a landlord's point of view is that s.55(1) HA 1980 introduced into RA

1977, as Case 19, a mandatory ground for possession. The ground is complex but required, in essence, the giving of notice in the prescribed form within certain time limits and that proceedings be commenced within three months of the expiry of that notice. The effect was to provide the landlord with a period of three months within each year during which possession proceedings could be brought under this ground (although the complex tactics of timing of service and length of notice could stretch the process of eviction over a much longer period).

2.04 *Use of assured and protected shorthold tenancies*

The HA 1980 assured tenancies were little used since they were restricted to newly built or converted dwellings and the landlord had to be 'approved'.

Protected shorthold tenancies appear to have achieved a larger measure of popularity. However, the requirements as to registration of a fair rent and the term of 1–5 years have hampered their wider usage.

Chapter 3

Assured Tenancies under the Housing Act 1988

3.01 Definition

By s.1(1) of the Act an assured tenancy is defined as:

'A tenancy under which a dwelling-house is let as a separate dwelling is for the purposes of this Act an assured tenancy if and so long as –

(a) the tenant or, as the case may be, each of the joint tenants is an individual; and
(b) the tenant or, as the case may be, at least one of the joint tenants occupies the dwelling-house as his only or principal home; and
(c) the tenancy is not one which, by virtue of subsection (2) or subsection (6) below, cannot be an assured tenancy.'

Thus, an assured tenancy is 'a tenancy under which a dwelling-house is let as a separate dwelling' and in respect of which the further considerations set out at s.1(1)(a)–(c) are also satisfied. We now turn to look at the constituent parts of this definition in more detail.

(1) 'Tenancy'

There must be a tenancy. An assured tenancy may be for a fixed term or for a periodic term so that the tenancy may be a fixed term tenancy, a periodic tenancy or a statutory periodic tenancy. A statutory periodic tenancy under the Act arises by the operation of s.5 (for which see page 19 below). By s.45 a fixed term tenancy is a tenancy which is not a periodic tenancy; 'tenancy' includes a sub-tenancy and an agreement for a tenancy or sub-tenancy, whilst 'tenant' includes a sub-tenant and any person deriving title under the original tenant or sub-tenant.

Since there must be a tenancy and the dwelling-house must be 'let', a licence cannot constitute an assured tenancy. In view of the importance of the distinction between a lease and a licence we give below, in Appendix I, an analysis of this subject. It should also be noted that licences which have in the past been restricted contracts (s.19 RA 1977) will not constitute, and cannot become, assured tenancies under the Act. They will, of course, retain the benefit of the Protection from Eviction Act 1977 ('PFEA 1977') as amended by the Act (see Chapter 6).

(2) 'Dwelling-house'

An assured tenancy must be of 'a' 'dwelling-house'. By s.45 'dwelling-house' may be a house or part of a house. Previous judicial interpretation of the expressions 'dwelling' and 'house' remain helpful. A house 'is a building for human habitation; especially a building that is the ordinary dwelling place of a family' (*Reed* v. *Hastings Borough Council* (1964) 62 LGR 588) and 'house' 'means a building which is constructed or adapted for use as or for the purposes of a dwelling' (*Ashbridge Investments Ltd* v. *MHLG* [1965] 1 WLR 1320). A building sub-divided into flats can remain a house. A flat is capable of being a dwelling-house by reason of s.45 of the Act.

'Dwelling' means a place in which all the major activities of life take place 'particularly sleeping, cooking and feeding' (*Wright* v. *Howell* (1948) 92 SJ 26), but mere sleeping is not enough (*Curl* v. *Angelo* [1948] 2 All ER 189).

It should also be noted that a 'dwelling-house' need not be constructed of bricks and mortar. All the circumstances must be considered and an immobilised caravan may qualify: *R* v. *Rent Officer of Nottingham Registration Area ex parte Allen* [1985] 2 EGLR 153.

(3) Dwelling-house may include 'other land'

Section 2(1)(a) provides that where a dwelling-house is let 'together with other land' then, if and so long as the 'main purpose' of the letting is the provision of a home for the tenant (or at least one of joint tenants), the other land is to be treated as part of the dwelling-house and an assured tenancy may be created (the land being treated as part of the dwelling-house).

Simply because a dwelling-house and land are let together does not mean that they are both subject to an assured tenancy. The 'main purpose' test must be satisfied. The land must be an adjunct of the dwelling-house and not *vice versa*: *Feyereisel* v. *Turnidge* [1952] 2 QB 29.

If and so long as the main purpose of the letting is not that of the provision of a home for the tenant (or one of joint tenants), then neither the land nor the dwelling-house will be treated as an assured tenancy: s.2(1)(b).

Furthermore, where the additional land is agricultural land exceeding two acres, the letting will not be assured: Schedule 1 para. 6.

(4) 'As a separate'

The letting must be 'as a separate' dwelling.

(a) The word 'as' requires that the purpose of the letting must be examined. The terms of the letting in so far as they relate to purpose are a primary (but not necessarily conclusive) consideration since all of the facts and circumstances must be examined.

(b) Since the letting must be as '*a*' separate dwelling, the letting must, at the time it takes place, be intended to be of a separate dwelling. Where a letting is composed of more than one dwelling (e.g. single letting of a block of flats) and intended to be used as more than one dwelling, it is not a tenancy of a separate dwelling: *Horford Investments Ltd* v. *Lambert* [1976] Ch 39; *St Catherine's College* v. *Dorling* [1980] 1 WLR 66; but more than one dwelling may be let as a single dwelling and fall within the definition: *Lower* v. *Porter* [1956] 1 QB 325.

(c) The word 'separate' means that the dwelling must be capable of use on its own with no sharing of 'living accommodation'. Living accommodation is a judicial creation and means accommodation used for sleeping, cooking and feeding but excludes a bathroom or lavatory since neither a bathroom nor lavatory is for living in.

However, the mere existence of shared accommodation which is also living accommodation will not necessarily prevent the tenancy from being 'separate' (and thus assured) where the tenant has exclusive use of some accommodation and shared use of other accommodation with persons other than the tenant's landlord: s.3. The question of shared accommodation and the provisions of s.3 of the Act are considered in more detail at page 36 and Appendix I below.

In addition s.4 of the Act provides that where an assured tenant sub-lets a part only of the dwelling-house, then as between the tenant and his landlord (or superior landlord), the letting continues to be that of an assured tenancy even though, as between the tenant and his sub-tenant, the terms of the sub-tenancy include the use of accommodation in common with others. Thus permitting a sub-tenant to share accommodation will not by itself cause the tenant to lose the security of an assured tenancy.

(5) 'If and so long as'

An assured tenancy only remains assured 'if and so long as' conditions (a)–(c) of s.1(1) are also fulfilled. Thus by s.1(1)(a) and (b) tenants must be individuals and the tenant (or at least one of two joint tenants) must occupy the dwelling-house as his only or principal home. If these conditions are not satisfied then the tenancy ceases to be assured and may be terminated by notice to quit without having to proceed under one of the grounds for possession under the Act (since those grounds consequently cease to apply).

It is not wholly clear from the expression 'if and so long as' whether, if a tenancy once ceases to be assured, it can later return to being an assured tenancy. The draftsman may have intended that such a conversion was impossible. However, it is difficult to construe 'if and so long as' in that way and the better view is that the tenancy is capable of losing and subsequently regaining assured status.

(6) 'Individual'

The tenant or 'each of the joint tenants' must be an 'individual', not a company. A landlord could therefore let to a company (provided that the letting is not a sham) of which the individual occupier was a shareholder and avoid the Act (see *Hilton* v. *Plustitle Ltd* [1988] 3 All ER 1051). Furthermore, a landlord could offer a joint tenancy to an individual and a company to avoid the Act – but see *Gisborne* v. *Burton* [1988] 3 WLR 921 which attempts to strike down agreements which are designed to deprive a tenant of statutory protection.

(7) 'Occupies'

A further requirement is that the tenant 'occupies' the dwelling-house. Problems may arise as to when a tenant ceases to occupy an assured tenancy. Although cases under RA 1977 may be helpful they should be treated with care since the requirement there is for occupation as 'his residence'.

Normal absences from the dwelling-house will almost certainly not result in cessation of occupation. Where a prolonged absence falls for consideration it is submitted that the question will be whether the tenant intended to return, and whether the dwelling remains the tenant's only or principal home. The tenant will have to show an intention to return coupled with physical evidence referrable to the dwelling-house in question to substantiate that intention, and that the dwelling-house is his only or principal home: see *Brown* v. *Brash* [1948] 2 KB 247; *Hoggett* v. *Hoggett* (1980) 39 P & CR 121; *Gofor Investments* v. *Roberts* (1975) 29 P & CR 366 and *Poland* v. *Cadogan* [1980] 3 All ER 544.

(8) 'Only or principal home'

The tenant must occupy the dwelling-house 'as his only or principal home'. This expression is not defined in the Act. It will be a question of fact as to whether the dwelling-house is that tenant's only or principal home. It is, however, clear that a tenant can only possess one such house. It follows that one of two joint tenants can possess another dwelling-house which is his or her principal home.

Finally, it should be noted that where a husband is a sole assured tenant and deserts his wife who remains at the tenancy, her occupation satisfies the occupancy requirement under the Act (s.1(6) of the Matrimonial Homes Act 1983 ('MHA 1983') as amended by paras 33 and 34 of Schedule 17 of the Act). By contrast, the divorcee may be left with no remedy since MHA 1983 requires that she be a spouse.

3.02   *Tenancies which cannot be assured tenancies*

By s.1(2) the following tenancies (set out in Schedule 1 paras 1–13 of the Act) cannot be assured tenancies:

(1) Tenancies entered into before 15 January 1989: (para. 1)

A tenancy entered into before 15 January 1989.

This paragraph also excludes tenancies entered into pursuant to contracts made before 15 January 1989 (see further at Chapter 5).

(2) Tenancies of dwelling-houses with high rateable values: (para. 2)

Tenancies of dwelling-houses having for the time being rateable values which in Greater London exceed £1500 and elsewhere exceed £750. Ascertainment of rateable value is covered in Part II of Schedule I.

It should be noted that the concept of 'the appropriate day' has been abandoned and that the valuation shown in the valuation list is the relevant consideration.

(3) Tenancies at a low rent: (para. 3)

Tenancies at no rent or a rent less than two-thirds of the rateable value for the time being of the dwelling-house.

In deciding what is rent for these purposes, sums expressed to be payable as rent in respect of rates, services, repairs, management, maintenance or insurance are to be disregarded unless the rent could not have been regarded by the parties to the tenancy as a part so payable: para. 3(2).

Rent must be quantifiable in money terms – a tenancy in exchange for services is not for rent: *Barnes* v. *Barratt* [1970] 2 QB 657. However, where an employee as part of his remuneration occupies rent-free premises provided by the employer but takes a reduction in wages, this reduction in wages represents his rent: *Montagu* v. *Browning* [1954] 1 WLR 1039.

(4) Business tenancies: (para. 4)

A business tenancy to which Part II LTA 1954 applies.

Part II LTA 1954 applies (subject to the provisions of that Act) to 'any tenancy where the property comprised in the tenancy is or includes premises which are occupied by the tenant, and are so occupied for the purposes of a business carried on by him or for those and other purposes': s.23(1) LTA 1954. For the purposes of s.23(1) business includes 'a trade, profession or employment and includes any activity carried on by a body of persons, whether corporate or unincorporate': s.23(2) LTA 1954.

Whilst use of the whole premises for business purposes clearly excludes the tenancy from the Act (for want of use as an only or principal home) a limited degree of business use will not necessarily have this effect: *Green* v. *Coggins* [1949] 2 All ER 815.

When deciding whether a tenancy is capable of attracting the protection of either the Act or LTA 1954, all of the circumstances must be examined. For example, keeping lodgers does not necessarily amount to business use. The degree of business use should be looked at – e.g. what are the commercial advantages for the tenant, the number of tenants and the rent paid? See: *Lewis* v. *Weldcrest* [1978] 1 WLR 1107; and *Abernethie* v. *Kleiman Ltd* [1970] 1 QB 10.

(5) Licensed premises: (para. 5)

On-licensed premises are not assured tenancies.

(6) Tenancies of agricultural land: (para. 6)

The head excludes a tenancy by which agricultural land, as defined by
s.26(3)(a) of the General Rate Act 1967 ('GRA 1967'), in excess of two
acres is let together with the dwelling-house. However, the purpose of
the letting should be examined. If the land is used principally for
recreation it may not be agricultural land.

(7) Tenancies of agricultural holdings: (para. 7)

This head excludes a tenancy (granted for example to a farm manager)
of a dwelling-house comprised in an agricultural holding (within the
meaning of the Agricultural Holdings Act 1986 'AHA 1986'), and
occupied by the person responsible for the control of the farming of
the holding.

(8) Lettings to students by specified educational institutions: (para. 8)

To qualify, the letting must be granted to a person who is pursuing, or
intends to pursue, a course of study provided by an educational
institution specified by the Secretary of State and the tenancy must be
granted by such an educational institution.

This exception does not apply to all student lettings but only to
those by educational institutions specified by the Secretary of State (SI
1988 No. 2236).

The letting that is excluded is that effected by such a qualifying
educational institution. A letting direct to students by a private
landlord will not fall within the exception. The letting to the institution
will not be assured because (*inter alia*) the tenant is not an individual.

(9) Holiday lettings: (para. 9)

A holiday letting is a tenancy the purpose of which is to confer on the
tenant the right to occupy the dwelling-house for a holiday.

'Holiday' is not defined in the Act and will remain a question of fact
but clearly the use must be for a genuine holiday. However, in
Buchmann v. *May* [1978] 2 All ER 993 the tenancy was expressly for

holiday occupation and it was held that the statement constituted *prima facie* evidence of the parties intentions – unless the tenant could prove the contrary.

(10) Resident landlords: (para. 10 (supplemented by Schedule 1 Part III))

In assessing whether a tenancy falls within this exemption:

(a) Decide whether the tenancy is of a purpose built block of flats. A block is purpose built if 'as constructed it contained and it contains' two or more flats. 'Flat' for these purposes means a dwelling-house forming part only of a building separated horizontally from another dwelling-house which forms part of the same building: see Schedule 1 Part III para. 22.

(b) If not a purpose built block of flats:

    (i) the dwelling-house must form part only of the building;

    (ii) the *grant* of the tenancy must have been made by an individual (or if by two or more persons, any of them) who at the time of the grant occupied as his only or principal home another dwelling-house which also forms part of the building; and

    (iii) since that grant the landlord must have been an individual (or if the landlord has been two or more persons, any of them) who at the time that he owned the reversion to the tenancy occupied as his only or principal home another dwelling-house which also formed part of the building.

(c) Where the dwelling-house does form part of a purpose built block of flats:

    (i) the dwelling-house must form part of the flat;

    (ii) the grant of the tenancy must have been made by an individual (or if by two or more persons, any of them) who at the time of the grant occupied as his only or principal home another dwelling-house which also formed part of the same flat; and

    (iii) since that grant the landlord must have been an individual (or if two or more persons, any of them) who at the time that he owned the reversion to the tenancy occupied as his only or principal house another dwelling-house which also formed part of the flat.

(d) Additionally (and this applies both to (b) and (c) above) the tenancy ('new tenancy') must not have been granted to a person (alone or with others) who was immediately before the grant a tenant under an assured tenancy ('former tenancy') of the same dwelling-house or of another dwelling-house forming part of the building in question by a landlord who was the same person both under the former tenancy and under the new tenancy.

The purpose of (d) above is to prevent a landlord who was not previously resident (but who wishes to become so to obtain possession) removing a tenant's assured status either by granting a new assured tenancy of the same dwelling-house or by moving the tenant to another flat or dwelling-house in the same building. However, this safeguard only applies where the tenant occupied under a former tenancy 'immediately' before the grant of the new tenancy.

The provisions of Schedule 1 para. 10(1)(c) refer to the 'interest of the landlord' under the tenancy, thus allowing sale of one resident landlord's interest to another without disturbing the residency exception. Part III of Schedule 1 governs allowable periods of non-occupation of the premises by the resident landlord.

(11) Crown tenancies (para. 11)

Crown tenancies (except where the interest is under the management of the Crown Estates Commissioners) and tenancies held by a government department.

(12) Certain local authority tenancies (para. 12)

Certain local and other authority tenancies (clearly enumerated in the paragraph) and shared ownership leases (under s.5A RA 1977 and created pursuant to para. 1 of Schedule 4 HPA 1986) (i.e. tenancies granted by a fully mutual housing association or a housing association trust).

(13) Certain transitional cases (para. 13)

These are:

(a) a protected tenancy under RA 1977
(b) a housing association tenancy under Part VI RA 1977
(c) a secure tenancy under Part IV HA 1985
(d) where a person is a protected occupier of a dwelling-house, within the meaning of RAA 1976.

3.03   Security of tenure

(1) Introduction

The underlying principle which confers security of tenure on the tenant is that neither an assured tenancy nor an assured shorthold tenancy can be brought to an end by the landlord unless the landlord has first served a notice seeking possession and subsequently obtained an order of the county court in accordance with the Act. It is convenient to look first at termination of the tenancy by the tenant and subsequently to examine the landlord's position. Thereafter, we will deal with the necessary court proceedings, the court's powers in those proceedings and the grounds upon which possession may be obtained.

(2) Termination of the tenancy by the tenant

In the hands of the tenant, the tenancy may be determined in accordance with the common law, so that if the tenancy is for a fixed term, the tenancy will only determine by effluxion of time or by surrender, unless the tenancy itself contains provision for its determination. If the tenancy is for a periodic term then a notice to quit must be given or a surrender made.

Since the Act seeks to prohibit the tenancy being brought to an end by the landlord otherwise than in accordance with the Act, antecedent agreements which might otherwise operate to terminate the tenancy are rendered either unenforceable or of no effect. Section 5(5) provides that if, on or before the date on which an assured tenancy is entered into (or a statutory periodic tenancy is deemed to have been granted by reason of s.5(3)(b) – see page 19 below), the prospective tenant either (a) agrees to do any act which would cause the assured tenancy to come to an end, or (b) executes, signs or gives any surrender notice to quit or other document which would have the same result, the agreement is unenforceable and any surrender or notice to quit etc. is of no effect.

(3) Termination of the tenancy by the landlord

The landlord wishing to terminate an assured tenancy must first establish whether the tenancy is for a periodic or a fixed term. The reason for this lies in s.5(1) which provides:

'An assured tenancy cannot be brought to an end by the landlord except by obtaining an order of the court in accordance with the following provisions of this Chapter or Chapter II below or, in the case of a fixed term tenancy which contains power for the landlord to determine the tenancy in certain circumstances, by the exercise of that power and, accordingly, the service by the landlord of a notice to quit shall be of no effect in relation to a periodic assured tenancy.'

So, if the assured tenancy in question is periodic an order of the court must be obtained; the service by the landlord of a notice to quit will have no effect.

Where the tenancy is for a fixed term which has not expired and the tenant is not in breach of the terms of the tenancy, the landlord must establish whether the tenancy contains a break clause. To have a break clause or clauses in an assured tenancy is perfectly valid and the reference in s.5(1) to 'power for the landlord to determine the tenancy in certain circumstances' can only refer to such a clause.

It certainly does not refer to a proviso for forfeiture or re-entry for breach of any term or condition of the tenancy: see s.45. If such a clause exists, and covers the situation in question, then its utilisation results in the creation of a statutory periodic tenancy: s.5(2). This may not help much since a court order is required to obtain possession against a tenant having the benefit of such a tenancy.

If the tenant is in breach, the landlord must utilise the proviso for forfeiture contained in the lease, bring possession proceedings and attempt to obtain a court order. However, in addition to establishing that one of the grounds for possession is available to him, he should first check that he is entitled to bring the tenancy to an end on the ground in question: s.7(6).

If the fixed term tenancy has expired by effluxion of time then once again a statutory periodic tenancy will arise by virtue of s.5(2), and a court order will be required to obtain possession as against the tenant. In this instance s.7(6) will not hamper the landlord since s.7(6) only restricts the court from making an order for possession 'to take effect at a time when' the dwelling-house is let on an 'assured fixed term tenancy'.

(4) The statutory periodic tenancy

(a) When does it arise?

A statutory periodic tenancy will arise where an assured fixed term tenancy comes to an end otherwise than in the circumstances mentioned in (b) below. If the statutory periodic tenancy arises then the tenant is entitled by that tenancy to remain in possession of the dwelling-house.

(b) When does it not arise?

A statutory periodic tenancy will not arise in the following circumstances:

(i) if the court makes an order for possession: s.5(2)(a)

(ii) if the assured tenancy is an assured shorthold tenancy and the tenancy is prevented from arising by reason of the provisions of Chapter II of the Act (see Chapter 4 below): s.5(2)

(iii) if the tenant surrenders or takes other similar action: s.5(2)(b)

(iv) if when the assured fixed term tenancy comes to an end the tenant is granted another tenancy 'of the same or substantially the same dwelling-house' as was let to him under the previous fixed term tenancy: s.5. Since this provision is satisfied where the new tenancy relates to the same or substantially the same dwelling-house, the new tenancy can otherwise be on different terms from the old. Thus, a fixed term might become periodic and the other terms of the tenancy may also be varied. The terms of such a new tenancy cannot be referred to a rent assessment committee (see page 37 below) since the tenancy will not be a statutory periodic tenancy but a new contractual assured tenancy.

(c) What are the terms of the statutory periodic tenancy?

A statutory periodic tenancy appears to be a genuine periodic tenancy. It should therefore be contrasted with the statutory tenancy which arises under the RA 1977 which is a personal right to remain. By s.5(3) it will:

(i) take effect in possession immediately on the coming to an end of the fixed term tenancy: s.5(3)(a)

(ii) be deemed to have been granted by the person who was the landlord of the fixed term tenancy at its expiry to the person who was then the tenant: s.5(3)(b)

(iii) comprise the same dwelling-house as was let under the fixed term tenancy: s.5(3)(c)
(iv) be periodic, the periods being the same as those in respect of which rent was payable under the fixed term tenancy: s.5(3)(d). Since the reference here is to 'payable' an annual rent of £1000 payable monthly results in a monthly tenancy
(v) otherwise (but subject to the terms of Chapter I of the Act) be on the same terms as the fixed term tenancy immediately before it came to an end save that any provision in the fixed term tenancy which allows for determination by the landlord or the tenant is of no effect whilst the statutory periodic tenancy remains assured: s.5(3)(e).

There are two particular points to note in respect of s.5(3)(e). Subject to the terms imposed by clauses 5(3)(a)–(d), the terms of the statutory periodic tenancy are the same as those of the preceding fixed term tenancy but with two exceptions. The first is that terms which are inconsistent with the provisions of Chapter 1 of the Act are not carried forward into the statutory tenancy. In this context reference should be made to s.15 of the Act which implies terms in respect of assignment and subletting into periodic (including statutory periodic) tenancies and also to s.16 which implies a right in favour of a landlord to carry out repairs in respect of periodic and statutory periodic tenancies: see page 40 below.

The second is that a provision for determination of the fixed term tenancy (i.e. a break clause) is of no effect whilst the statutory periodic tenancy remains assured. It seems that such a provision is carried forward into the statutory periodic tenancy but remains of no effect unless and until the tenancy in question loses its assured status.

(5) Obtaining possession

(a) The general principles

Possession proceedings are to be commenced in the appropriate county court: s.40(1). If the action is commenced in the High Court then the plaintiff will recover only the costs that he would have obtained had the action been commenced in the county court (s.40(4)) unless the purpose of taking proceedings in the High Court was to enable them to be joined with proceedings already before the High Court: s.40(5).

The court may only make an order for possession of an assured tenancy on one of the grounds for possession specified in Schedule 2 of the Act. This principle does not apply to a mortgagee who has made a loan secured on the tenant's interest under an assured tenancy: s.7(1).

The grounds specified are either mandatory (Part I of Schedule 2) or discretionary (Part II of Schedule 2). Where a mandatory ground is established the court is required to make an order (s.7(3)) and if a discretionary ground is established then the court may make an order for possession 'if it considers it reasonable to do so'.

However, where the tenancy in question is an assured fixed term tenancy whose term has not come to an end, there is a further requirement which must be satisfied, whether the ground for possession is mandatory or discretion only. By s.7(6) the court is prohibited from making an order for possession in respect of such a tenancy unless the terms of the tenancy specifically provide for termination of the tenancy on the ground in question, *and* the ground established is mandatory ground 2 or 8 or any of the discretionary grounds (other than numbers 9 or 16). This point must be appreciated by the draftsman of a fixed term assured tenancy.

The requirement that the court may only make an order for possession under one of the discretionary grounds 'if it considers it reasonable to do so' requires discussion. The equivalent reference in the Rent Act 1977 at s.98(1) is 'unless the court considers it reasonable' to do so, so that the circumstances considered under the Rent Act 1977 are clearly relevant here. The question of reasonableness is a separate matter for the court and must be considered by it separately. It is the reasonableness of the order for possession that has to be considered, not the reasonableness of the landlord's requirement for possession. In deciding the issue of reasonableness the court must consider all the circumstances as they exist at the date of the hearing: *Cumming* v. *Danson* [1942] 2 All ER 653. A comprehensive list of examples illustrating circumstances in which it was reasonable to grant possession can be found in R.E. Megarry's *The Rent Acts* (11th Edition, 1988, at pp.387–93).

(b) The procedural requirements

The court may not entertain proceedings for possession of an assured tenancy unless the landlord (or at least one of joint landlords) has served a notice in the prescribed form (see SI 1988 No. 2203, Form No. 3, reproduced in Appendix III below) seeking possession and has begun the proceedings within the time limits mentioned below: s.8(1)(a). In certain circumstances the court may dispense with the requirement for notice where it considers it 'just and equitable to do so': s.8(1)(b).

The notice seeking possession must:

(i) specify the ground, and particulars of that ground, which are intended to be relied upon (but the court may give leave to alter or add to the grounds specified): s.8(2)

(ii) state that the landlord intends to begin proceedings for possession upon one or more of the grounds specified: s.8(3)(a)

(iii) state that proceedings will not begin earlier than a date specified in the notice nor later than 12 months from the date of service of the notice.

The minimum period from the date of service of the notice that may be specified for the purpose of commencement of proceedings is two weeks unless the notice alleges any of grounds 1, 2, 5, 6, 7, 9 or 16. If any of these grounds are specified the minimum period becomes two months, unless the tenancy is periodic, in which case the minimum period (if longer than two months) becomes the earliest date on which the tenancy could be brought to an end by notice to quit given on the same day as the date of service of the notice. Thus a quarterly tenancy requires a quarter's notice.

Where a notice under section 8 is served at a time when the dwelling-house is let on an assured fixed term tenancy, or is served after that tenancy has expired, but relates to events which occurred during that tenancy, the notice is effective even though the tenant may in the meantime have become a tenant under a statutory periodic tenancy: s.8(6).

As mentioned above, the court has power to dispense with the requirements of notice where it considers it 'just and equitable' to do so (s.8(1)(b)), although it cannot exercise this discretion if ground 8 (rent arrears of at least three months at the date of the notice and hearing) is alleged: s.8(5).

'Just and equitable' will be a question of fact in each case. However, it seems unlikely that a court will waive the notice requirements unless the tenant has been clearly forewarned of the proceedings and no possible injustice has been committed by the failure to serve the notice.

(6) The extended discretion of the court

The court has a discretion, where a claim for possession is based on a discretionary ground (and does not relate to an assured shorthold tenancy) to adjourn the proceedings (s.9(1)); and on the making of an order for possession or before its execution has power to stay or suspend execution of the order or to postpone the date of possession for such period or periods as it thinks just: s.9(2).

Where the court exercises its discretion under either s.9(1) or s.9(2) it must impose conditions (if applicable) for the payment of arrears of rent and rent or mesne profits (unless to do so would cause exceptional hardship or otherwise be unreasonable) and it has a wide discretion to impose other conditions where appropriate: s.9(3).

Where those conditions are met the court has power to discharge or rescind any order made: s.9(4). By s.9(5) the spouse or former spouse of a tenant who has rights of occupation under the Matrimonial Homes Act 1983, and who remains in occupation of the dwelling-house, has preserved to her the same rights to apply for a stay, postponement, suspension or adjournment as she would have had, had she been the assured tenant, so that for this purpose occupation by a non-tenant spouse is deemed occupation by a tenant-spouse.

3.04   *The grounds for possession*

The relevant text of the Act is printed in Appendix II of this book and the grounds are set out in Schedule 2 of the Act. Little is gained by laboriously setting out each ground. We therefore comment on the salient points of each, dealing with the grounds in the order in which they appear in the Act.

(1) The requirement for notice in relation to grounds 1–5

Each of grounds 1–5 require that notice be given by the landlord to the tenant of any intention to use the ground in question 'not later than the beginning of the tenancy'. The relevant notice provisions are contained in s.7(5) and Schedule 2 Part IV and may be briefly summarised thus:

(a) No form of notice is prescribed but the notice must be given not later than the day on which the tenancy is entered into: Schedule 2 Part IV para. 11.
(b) Where the tenancy is to be granted by joint landlords at least one of them must give the notice: Schedule 2 Part IV para. 7.
(c) Where a notice has once been validly given in respect of a tenancy no further notice need be given prior to the beginning of a subsequent tenancy provided that (i) the subsequent tenancy arose immediately after the previous tenancy came to an end, (ii) the tenant of the subsequent tenancy was also the tenant of the previous tenancy, (iii) both tenancies are of

substantially the same dwelling-house: Schedule 2 Part IV para. 8(1) and (2).

The wording of the schedule is not completely free from doubt and it will be wise (where possible) for the notice to be given on each grant and regrant of any tenancy.

The principle set out in Schedule 2 Part IV paras 8(1) and (2) will, however, not apply to a later tenancy where the landlord gives notice before the beginning of that tenancy that possession will not be recovered under the ground in question: Schedule 2 Part IV para. 8(3).

(d) There are specific additional provisions in relation to ground 1 (Schedule 2 Part IV para. 9) and grounds 3 and 4 (Schedule 2 Part IV para. 10) which should be noted where relevant.

(2) The mandatory grounds

Ground 1: (Available where (a) landlord previously occupied the dwelling-house as his only or principal home or (b) where landlord now requires the dwelling-house as his or his spouse's only or principal home and (c) notice has been given)

The ground in fact creates two potential methods of obtaining possession depending upon different sets of circumstances. Under para. (a) possession may be obtained where the landlord seeking possession has occupied the dwelling-house as his only or principal home (for which expression see page 11 above) before the beginning of the tenancy. There is no stipulation as to the period of such occupancy or even a requirement as to exactly when it took place – merely that it should have taken place before the beginning of the tenancy and have been in respect of the dwelling-house for which possession is sought.

Under para. (b) a landlord may obtain possession where he requires the dwelling-house as either his or his spouse's only or principal home. Para. (b) will not therefore assist the landlord who wishes to take possession in order to sell immediately.

However, possession cannot be obtained under (b) where the landlord seeking possession (or in the case of joint landlords *either* of them) acquired the 'reversion on the tenancy for money or money's worth'. The intention is to distinguish between the person who acquired the dwelling-house with vacant possession and then let it (who will be unaffected) and the person who acquires the dwelling-house subject to the tenancy who may be affected. Equally a person who purchases the reversion on the tenancy with the benefit of the notice will not be able to obtain vacant possession.

In either case the relevant notice must have been given in writing before the date that the tenancy is entered into unless the court considers it just and equitable to dispense with this requirement.

In any use of its discretion the court must consider all of the circumstances and the crucial point will be whether the tenant fully understood whether or not he had security of tenure: *Bradshaw* v. *Baldwin-Wiseman* (1985) 49 P & CR 382.

The minimum period of notice for possession under s.8(4) is two months.

Ground 2: (Mortgagee's right of possession dependent upon the mortgage having been created before the tenancy and notice having been given)
This ground only applies where the mortgage of the dwelling-house was created before the tenancy. Unless dispensed with under the just and equitable ground, the notice must have been given by the landlord (not the landlord's mortgagee) before the tenancy was entered into. Where the notice has been validly given, any prospective mortgagee of a dwelling-house which is already charged and subject to a tenancy should consider taking a transfer of the existing charge (whether or not in addition to fresh security) to preserve this ground.

The mortgage should contain a covenant on the part of the mortgagor not to let without consent and to give notice under this ground where appropriate. Where the letting has been effected without the consent of the mortgagee, the mortgagee may be able to treat the tenant as a trespasser: *Dudley and District Building Society* v. *Emerson* [1949] Ch 707.

By reason of s.7(6) this ground should be considered for inclusion in any fixed term tenancy. Where possession proceedings are commenced, the minimum notice period under s.8(4) is two months.

Ground 3: (Alternation of fixed term letting with holiday letting, notice having been given)
This is *not* an exemption for holiday letting, since genuine holiday lets are not assured tenancies. The intention is to permit a landlord to grant short fixed term lettings and holiday lettings of the same dwelling-house.

The dwelling-house must in the 12 month period preceding the grant of the fixed term tenancy have been occupied 'under a right to occupy it for a holiday', so that there must have been a genuine holiday let in that period.

If the ground is to be used, notice must be given not later than the date the tenancy is entered into. In an action for possession the minimum notice period under s.8(3) is two weeks.

Ground 4: (Alternation of letting with student letting, notice having been given)

A tenancy within para. 8 of Schedule 1 is a tenancy which is granted to a person who is pursuing, or intending to pursue, a course of study provided by a specified educational institution *and is so granted* by that institution or by another specified institution or body of persons. Thus to qualify, the letting to the student *must* be a letting by that body and not by a landlord who does not qualify as a specified body under that paragraph.

The landlord must have given the requisite notice before the tenancy was entered into. Where possession proceedings are commenced the minimum period is two weeks: s.8(3).

Ground 5: (Dwelling-house available for occupation by a minister of religion and notice given)

Once again the requirement that notice be given is absolute. The minimum period for the purposes of possession proceedings under s.8(3) is two weeks.

Ground 6: (The landlord intends to demolish or reconstruct the whole or a substantial part or to carry out substantial works which cannot for specified reasons be carried out without possession of the assured tenancy)

The first point to check is that the ground is available to the landlord under para. (b) *and* (c) of ground 6. To qualify, the landlord must have acquired his interest before the grant of the tenancy or (if the landlord's interest was in existence at the time of the grant) then neither the landlord seeking possession (or in the case of joint landlords any of them), nor any other person who has acquired that interest since that time, may have acquired it by purchase or for moneys worth.

The title to the landlord's interest must be carefully investigated to establish that these conditions are met. If they are not, the landlord may be tempted to offer the tenant a new tenancy on attractive terms. A tenant should hesitate before accepting, since to do so may correct the defect and permit the landlord to proceed.

The second point to check is that the tenancy is assured but that it did not come into being as a consequence of a succession to a Rent Act protected or statutory tenancy.

Assuming these requirements are met, the first step for the landlord is to show at the hearing that he 'intends to demolish or reconstruct the whole or a substantial part of the dwelling-house or to carry out substantial works on the dwelling-house or any part thereof or any building of which it forms part'. If the authorities on the meaning of s.30(1) (f) LTA 1954 prove to be of help in interpreting this then the landlord must demonstrate a firm settled intention to effect the works and on the balance of probabilities the ability to implement them: *Cunliffe* v. *Goodman* [1950] 2 KB 237; *Fisher* v. *Taylors Furnishing Stores Ltd* [1956] 2 QB 78; and *Reohorn* v. *Barry Corporation* [1956] 2 All ER 742.

The landlord must then show that the work 'cannot reasonably be carried out without the tenant giving up possession of the dwelling-house' for any of the specific reasons at para. (a). If the nature of the works constitutes reconstruction or the carrying out of 'substantial works' then, if the ground is to be used successfully, prior negotiations with the tenant(s) affected may be essential since otherwise a tenant can effectively use sub-paragraphs (a)(i) or (a)(ii) as a defence.

The minimum period of notice under s.8(4) is two months. Where a landlord obtains possession, removal expenses are available to the tenant under s.11 of the Act but no compensation is payable.

Ground 7: (Recovery of periodic tenancy within 12 months of tenant's death)

It should be noted that the ground is not available to a landlord where the successor to the tenancy is the deceased tenant's spouse and the conditions of s.17(1) are met: see page 40 below. Where the ground is available the minimum period of notice under s.8(4) is two months.

Ground 8: (Rent arrears of three months)

In practice, ground 8 may prove difficult to establish since the minimum period of arrears must exist both at the date of service of the s.8 notice and at the date of the hearing. For this reason grounds 10 and 11 should also be specified. The minimum period of notice under s.8(3) for each of grounds 8, 10 and 11 is two weeks. By s.8(5) the court cannot waive the notice requirement under s.8(3). By reason of s.7(6) consideration should be given to specifying this ground in any assured fixed term tenancy.

(3) The discretionary grounds

As discussed at page 21 above these grounds empower a court to order possession 'if it considers it reasonable to do so': s.7(3). The minimum period of notice of proceedings is two weeks (s.8(3)) unless either of ground 9 or 16 is relied upon, when the period is two months: s.8(4).

Ground 9: (Suitable alternative accommodation is available for the tenant or will be available for him when the order for possession takes effect)

The ground will be established where the alternative accommodation is 'suitable' and available for the tenant against whom possession is sought no later than the moment when the order takes effect.

By s.7(5), Schedule 2 Part III defines 'suitable alternative accommodation'. A certificate of the local housing authority stating that they will provide alternative accommodation by a date specified in the certificate is conclusive. In the absence of this the landlord has three principal hurdles to overcome and in some instances a fourth.

The first is the nature of the prospective tenancy. This must either be an assured tenancy (not being an assured shorthold tenancy or an assured tenancy where notice is given under any of grounds 1–5) or a letting (such as a secure letting under the Housing Act 1985) which confers security equal to that of an assured tenancy: Schedule 2, Part III para. 2.

The second is that the accommodation must be reasonably suitable to the needs of the tenant *and* his family as regards proximity to place of work: Schedule 2, Part III para. 3(1).

The third requires the accommodation offered to be either similar as regards 'rental and extent' to equivalent local housing authority accommodation *or* reasonably suitable to the means of the tenant and the needs of the tenant and his family as regards extent and character: Schedule 2, Part III para. 3(1)(a) and (b) and 3(2). 'Means' clearly relates to rent and other outgoings, whilst 'needs' probably means 'housing needs': see *Hill* v. *Rochard* [1983] 1 WLR 478. 'Character' includes a reference to the situation of the accommodation so that a move from a quiet street to a noisy road with a fish and chip shop next door was not a move to suitable alternative accommodation: *Redspring* v. *Francis* [1973] 1 WLR 134.

Fourth, where furniture was provided under the assured tenancy to be possessed, furniture which is either 'similar' to that previously supplied or reasonably suitable to the needs of the tenant and his family must be supplied in the alternative accommodation. Where the order is granted removal expenses may be obtained: s.11.

Ground 10: (Rent arrears)

Under ground 10 some rent must be 'lawfully due from the tenant' and unpaid both on the date that proceedings are begun and at the date of the notice under s.8 (unless the court waives the notice requirement).

Ground 11: (Persistent delay in the payment of rent)
In the absence of ground 11 the persistent bad payer is able to escape the consequences of ground 8 (which requires at least three months' arrears) and ground 10 (which requires arrears at specified moments). However the need to show that the tenant has 'persistently delayed' suggests a long history of delayed payments evidenced by detailed records.

Ground 12: (Breach of an obligation of the tenancy other than rent)
It seems likely that, in practice, this will not be pleaded as a principal ground for possession but as an additional ground.

Ground 13: (Neglect causing deterioration)
The requirement is for the condition of the dwelling-house or of any 'common parts' (as defined) to 'deteriorate'. A mere breach of covenant may not result in deterioration, e.g. failure to paint in a specified colour. In multi-tenanted properties establishing precisely which tenant committed which act may prove difficult.

Ground 14: (Conduct which is a nuisance/annoyance or conviction for use of the dwelling-house for illegal or immoral purposes)
There are two distinct limbs to ground 14. The first requires that the tenant (or other resident) be guilty of conduct which amounts to a nuisance or annoyance to adjoining occupiers. 'Nuisance' is used in its dictionary sense whilst annoyance may be given a broader meaning than nuisance and means annoyance to the reasonable, not over-sensitive person: *Tod-Heatly* v. *Benham* (1888) 40 ChD 80.

Under the second limb the tenant (or other resident) must be convicted of 'using' the dwelling-house for immoral or illegal purposes. In order to establish the ground the dwelling-house itself must have been used for the crime so as to associate the two: *Abrahams* v. *Wilson* [1971] 2 QB 88.

Ground 15 (Deterioration of furniture provided for use due to ill-treatment)
A landlord wishing to use this ground should possess a detailed inventory, supplemented by photographs, and drawn up before the grant of the tenancy in question to illustrate the extent of the ill-treatment relied upon.

Ground 16: (Termination of the employment which gave rise to the letting)

The original letting to the tenant must have been 'in consequence of his employment' which implies that it must have been a necessary or integral part of it. Whilst the landlord seeking possession only has to show that the employment of the tenant has 'ceased' (and not that he intends to relet to a new employee), the separate reasonableness requirement may in practice require the landlord to declare, and justify, his intended use of the property.

(4) Removal expenses

By s.11 where possession of an assured tenancy is ordered under ground 6 (demolition and reconstruction) or ground 9 (suitable alternative accommodation) the landlord must pay the tenant's reasonable expenses in moving from the dwelling-house. If agreement is not reached between the parties as to the amount of the expenses, the court may determine the amount.

(5) Misrepresentation

Section 12 provides that where a landlord obtains possession by 'misrepresentation or concealment of material facts', the court may order the landlord to pay to the tenant a sum that is sufficient compensation for damages and loss sustained as a result of that order.

3.05   *Rent and rent review*

The Act is essentially a decontrolling measure leaving the landlord free to extract a market rent or, for that matter, any rent he can obtain. It follows that the interference with rent fixing is slight in comparison with the Rent Act regime, but there are complex procedural provisions which will be dictated by the status of the tenancy.

(1) Rent review

When a property is let on an assured tenancy, the fair rent system under the RA 1977 does not apply and can be disregarded. During the currency of a contract for an assured tenancy, that contract is likely to govern the provisions as to rent. In the case of a fixed term tenancy, this will bind the parties for the currency of the term fixed. The tenant will be able to insist on the rent level laid down in the contract, and any attempt by the landlord to vary unilaterally the contract, even by reference to a rent assessment committee, can be resisted. The landlord may insert a rent review clause into the lease, but, whether or not a fixed term assured tenancy contains a rent review clause, rent will be governed by the contract and not by the s.13 rent fixing provisions which are considered below.

At common law the landlord of a periodic tenancy has an effective means of increasing rent at any time. It is possible to determine the tenancy by serving a notice to quit, and thereafter let at a higher rent level. Because the security of tenure provisions in the Act restrict the landlord's ability to follow this course of action the contract may provide for rent review. Where the review clause in an assured tenancy constitutes a clause 'for the time being binding on the tenant, under which the rent for a particular period of the tenancy will or may be greater than the rent for an earlier period' (s.13(1)(b)) then it will govern future rent increases. Landlords wishing to avoid the s.13 procedures, outlined in the following section, should use an effective rent review clause.

(2) Rent increases under the Act

Other than for fixed term tenancies and periodic tenancies with a binding rent increase provision, a statutory process for increase of rent will apply. This is dealt with in s.13, which details the notice procedures and applies to rent increases under other assured periodic tenancies including statutory periodic tenancies. It is necessary to make some differentiation between the application of the procedure to periodic and statutory periodic tenancies.

In the case of the latter, the landlord will be able to propose a rent increase upon a statutory periodic tenancy arising whether by the expiry of a fixed term tenancy (see s.5(2)) or via transitional provisions upon succession to a tenancy previously protected under the Rent Acts (see Chapter 5). In the case of an assured periodic tenancy without provision for rent review, the rent cannot be increased under s.13 until the first anniversary of the date upon which the tenancy began. Thereafter, where the rent has been increased previously by a s.13 notice or a s.14 determination, future increases can take effect at the earliest upon the first anniversary of that increase taking effect.

To obtain a rent increase the landlord must serve a notice in the prescribed form proposing a new rent to take effect at the beginning of a new period of the tenancy as specified in the notice (s.13(2)). That period cannot begin earlier than 12 months after the date when the first period began, and, in addition, it must not commence before a minimum period following the service of the notice. The minimum period depends on the length of the tenancy (s.13(3)):

(a) if it is a yearly tenancy the minimum period is six months
(b) if the tenancy is for less than a month, the minimum period is one month; and
(c) in any other case, it is a period equal to the period of the tenancy.

Section 13 makes provision for the landlord only to apply for a rent increase. There is no parallel provision enabling a tenant to serve a notice requesting a reduction in rent. The notice must be in the prescribed form, and the relevant form (SI 1988/2203 Form 5) is reproduced in Appendix III of this book. As that form states, it applies only to s.13 increases and not where a rent adjustment is proposed for a statutory periodic tenancy solely because of a change of terms under s.6(2) of the Act (see page 170).

The notice offers certain information to the tenant, and in particular draws attention to the time limits and suggests that legal advice be sought. It points to the right of the tenant to refer the matter to the rent assessment committee ('RAC') (see below and Chapter 7).

Once a valid notice has been served the new rent will take effect on the date specified in the notice, *unless* before the beginning of the new period:

(a) the tenant refers the matter to the RAC (s.13(4)(a)); or
(b) the landlord and tenant agree on a rent variation different from that proposed (s.13(4)(b)); or
(c) the landlord and tenant agree not to vary the rent (s.13(5)).

It will therefore be vitally important for the tenant to refer the matter to the RAC. In the event of a failure to do so, the landlord will in effect be able to impose a new rent unilaterally. In practice many landlords may by-pass RACs by negotiating a rent with the tenant in advance of the service of a s.13 notice, and by explaining the necessity for, and content of, that notice in advance of any proposed increase.

If the tenant wishes to object to an increase proposed by a s.13 notice, then the onus is on the tenant to refer the matter to the RAC within the prescribed timescale (see above). The relevant form is reproduced in Appendix III (SI 1988/2203 Form 6). Most of the information with which the RAC will work initially (e.g. to decide jurisdictional issues) is contained in this form.

Once a reference is made the RAC is required to determine the rent at which it considers that the dwelling-house might reasonably be expected to be let in the open market by a willing landlord under an assured tenancy (s.14(1)):

(a) which is a periodic tenancy on the same periodic basis as that to which the notice relates
(b) which begins at the beginning of a new period specified in the notice
(c) the terms of which (other than as to rent) are the same as those of the tenancy to which the notice relates; and
(d) taking into account any notices served under Schedule 2 grounds 1–5 (see page 24 above).

There are a number of factors which the committee must disregard in making its determination (s.14(2)). These follow closely provisions relating to business tenancies under s.34 LTA 1954. They are:

(a) Any effect on the rent of giving a tenancy to a sitting tenant.
(b) Any increase in the value of the dwelling which is attributable to a tenant's improvement. In order to be relevant here an improvement must be carried out *other than* in pursuance of an obligation to the tenant's immediate landlord. This can include the situation where that obligation is subject none the less to the consent of the landlord. The effect is that where the tenant makes improvements voluntarily (or where the law construes such improvements as 'voluntary') their effect must be disregarded.
   In addition the requirements of s.14(3) must be met. That is, the improvement must have been carried out during the current tenancy (and not, for example pursuant to a licence preceding the grant of the tenancy: *Euston Centre Properties* v. *H. & J. Wilson* (1982) 262 EG 1079. If not carried out during the tenancy to which the notice relates the following conditions must be met:

   (i) the improvement must have been completed not more than 21 years before the date of service of the notice; and
   (ii) the premises at all times since the improvement was made until the date of service of the notice must have been let under an assured tenancy; and
   (iii) if during any of the above periods the assured tenancy

came to an end, the then tenant (or if joint tenants, at least one of them) remained in possession.

It will be apparent from the above discussion that there is no requirement that the relevant improvements be carried out by the tenant. For some relevant background to the equivalent LTA 1954 provisions, see *Re 'Wonderland' Cleethorpes* [1965] AC 58 and section 1 of the Law of Property Act 1969 ('LPA 1969').

(c) Any reduction in value of the house attributable to a breach of an obligation under the tenancy by the tenant.

There seems to be no necessity to make allowance for the landlord's failure to repair (c.f. *Fawke* v. *Viscount Chelsea* [1980] QB 441 decided under s.34 LTA 1954). Indeed if the tenant undertakes repair in the absence of the landlord's fulfilment of an obligation, the value of that repair would seem to accrue to the landlord.

For the above purposes 'rent' does not include payments for services where those payments are by way of a variable service charge (s.14(4)). (The reasonableness of such a charge is governed by s.12 LTA 1985). Subject to this 'rent' includes payments for furniture and services (as defined) but is determined by the RAC at a figure which is exclusive of rates (s.14(5)). Therefore if under the tenancy agreement the landlord is responsible for rates, these may be added to the amount determined by the RAC.

(3) Section 6 procedure under statutory periodic tenancies

The ss.13/14 procedure is very different from the s.6 procedure for alteration of terms under statutory periodic tenancies. Under s.6 (which is dealt with in more detail at page 37 below) the rent may only be increased to take account of an adjustment of other terms under the tenancy. Under ss.13 and 14 the RAC may only adjust the rent – not the other terms.

It is possible for two references to be made to the RAC – one under s.6 and the other under ss.13/14. If the RAC hears both references at the same time (it is not obliged to do so) it shall first make a determination on the s.6 reference before making a determination on the s.13 reference, so taking into account the new terms when deciding the new rent (s.14(6)).

(4) Effect of rent assessment committee determination

Unless the landlord and tenant agree otherwise, the rent determined by the RAC is to be operative from the beginning of the period specified in the notice (s.14(7)). However, if it appears to the RAC that that would cause undue hardship to the tenant, then it may specify a later date which must not be later than the date of its decision. This may be useful in the event of a backlog of claims before the RAC, giving rise to a long delay between the landlord's specified date and the RAC determination. Advisers for both sides may wish to address the RAC on this issue.

(5) Agreement and withdrawal

Again, it is provided that the RAC is not required to continue with a determination if the landlord and tenant give written notice that they no longer require such a determination (s.14(8)). Even after the determination, the parties may agree to vary the rent so that any level fixed by the RAC is *not* a legal maximum. Presumably, the ability of a landlord to conclude an agreement beyond the rent level fixed folowing the ss.13/14 procedure will depend upon the ease with which the landlord can seek to recover possession.

For a fuller review of the powers of RACs see Chapter 7.

(6) Rent books

A tenant under a weekly assured tenancy must be provided with a rent book (s.4 of the Landlord and Tenant Act 1985, 'LTA 1985'). The form of rent book notice is prescribed by SI 1982 No. 1474 and SI 1988 No. 2198 (s.(1) LTA 1985 and para. 67 of Schedule 17 HA 1988).

3.06   *Other matters relating to assured tenancies*

(1) Shared accommodation

By s.3(1) where a tenant has the exclusive occupation of accommodation (described in the section as 'the separate accommodation') and:

(i) the terms of the tenancy governing the separate accommodation include the use of other accommodation shared with others (excluding the landlord); and

(ii) by reason only of this the separate accommodation is not an assured tenancy

then the separate accommodation is deemed to be an assured tenancy. It should be noted at once that it is the terms of the tenancy that are the determining factor.

The reasoning behind the inclusion of this section is that under s.1 a tenancy will not qualify as an assured tenancy unless it is of (*inter alia*) a dwelling-house let as a 'separate' dwelling. Thus it must be capable of use as a single unit without recourse to sharing of 'living accommodation'. Section 3 has therefore been enacted to overcome an obvious means of circumventing the Act, and the meaning of the expression 'living accommodation' for the purposes of the section is spelt out in these terms in s.3(5).

By s.3(2) where it is necessary to make an apportionment under Part II of Schedule 1 for the purpose of determining the rateable value of the separate accommodation, regard shall be had in determining that value to the use of the shared accommodation.

Whilst the tenant is in possession of the separate accommodation any term of the tenancy providing for, or terminating, or modifying the right of the tenant to the use of the shared accommodation which is also living accommodation shall be of no effect: s.3(3). However a provision in the tenancy agreement which entitles other persons to use the accommodation or which provides for an increase in the number of those persons is effective: s.3(4).

Section 10 of the Act contains certain special provisions relating to tenancies falling within s.3. First, by s.10(2) the court cannot order that possession be granted of shared accommodation unless at the same time possession is ordered of the separate accommodation.

Section 10(3), however, gives the landlord the right to make application to the court for an order determining the use of the shared (but not living) accommodation or modifying the use of shared accommodation. On such an application the court may (if it thinks it just) either:

(a) terminate the right of the tenant to use the whole or any part of the shared accommodation which is not living accommodation (as defined in s.3(5)); or
(b) modify the right of the tenant to use the whole or any part of the shared accommodation.

However, the court has no power to make any order under s.10(3) unless that power exists 'under the terms of the tenancy': s.10(4). Thus even though a term of the tenancy, for example, terminating the use of shared accommodation is ineffective under s.3(3), it must be included lest the landlord needing to have that flexibility is unable to ask the court to exercise its discretion under s.10(3).

(2) The section 6 procedure

The section is available to both a landlord and a tenant of a statutory periodic tenancy (whether or not that tenancy is assured) arising by virtue of s.5: s.5(7). It enables either party to make proposals for a variation in the terms of the statutory periodic tenancy which are implied by s.5(3)(e) (other than as to the amount of rent). Unacceptable proposals are referable to an RAC which is required to make a determination.

There are a number of limitations on its operation which should be noted, namely:

(a) It applies only to a statutory periodic tenancy arising by s.5 (i.e. former fixed term tenants).
(b) It does not apply to a statutory periodic tenancy at a time when it cannot be assured because it falls within paras 11 or 12 of Schedule 1 to the Act (Crown and local authority tenancies).
(c) The proposals which may be considered are terms (other than rent) implied by s.5(3)(e) and no other terms.
(d) It may not be used to vary rent (for which see ss.13 and 14) except where the rental increase or decrease is an adjustment consequent on a variation of the terms of the tenancy.

The procedure may be summarised as follows:

(a) Not later than the first anniversary of the day on which the fixed term tenancy ('former tenancy') came to an end either the landlord or the tenant may serve on the other a notice in the prescribed form (SI 1988 No. 2203 Form 1), proposing:

   (i) a variation in the terms of the statutory periodic tenancy implied by s.5(3)(e) ('implied terms'); and
   (ii) (if appropriate) an adjustment in the rent to reflect those terms: s.6(2).

(b) The landlord or tenant who receives such a notice has three months (commencing with the date of service) to refer the notice to an RAC. That reference must be in the prescribed form: see SI 1988 No. 2203 Form 2: s.6(3)(a). If that reference is not made, then with effect from the date specified in the notice (which may not be earlier than a period of three months from the date of service of the notice) the variation and adjustment (if any) proposed takes effect automatically s.6(3)(b).

(c) If a notice is referred to an RAC, the RAC is required to 'determine' whether the proposed terms or some other terms are terms which might reasonably be expected to be found in an assured periodic tenancy of the dwelling-house in question. The RAC is required to assume that the periodic tenancy in question began on the date that the former tenancy expired, and was granted by a willing landlord on the same terms as those of the statutory periodic tenancy at the time of the RAC's consideration, except in so far as those terms relate to the terms proposed by the notice: s.6(4).

(d) The RAC is then required to state the date upon which the terms determined by it are to become the terms of the statutory periodic tenancy and to state the amount of any consequential variation in rent: s.6(7).

In addition, the RAC has the power when determining the terms of a statutory periodic tenancy under s.6(4) to specify an adjustment of rent under that tenancy: s.6(5). In making a determination under s.6(4) or an adjustment under s.6(5) the RAC is to disregard any effect on the terms or the amount of the rent attributable to the granting of a tenancy to a sitting tenant: s.6(6).

A determination of the RAC under s.6(7) is binding on the landlord and tenant unless both of them agree that they will not be bound by it: s.6(7). This avoids both parties being disappointed by a compromise solution put forward by the RAC. Furthermore if both the landlord and tenant give written notice to the RAC that they no longer require a determination, or if the tenancy in question comes to an end, then the RAC has the power to cease the determination: s.6(8).

By s.41 an RAC can require that a landlord or tenant supply it with such information as it may reasonably require for the purposes of its determination. The form of notice is set out at SI 1988 No. 2203 Form 9 reproduced in Appendix III of this book and must be answered within 14 days of service. Failure to comply could result in a conviction and fine in the magistrate's court.

(3) Alienation

(a) Fixed term tenancies

A *fixed term* assured tenancy is freely assignable unless there is any provision in the lease to the contrary. If the landlord's consent is required then s.19 of the Landlord and Tenant Act 1927 ('LTA 1927') (whereby it is implied that consent is not to be unreasonably withheld) applies.

(b) Assured periodic tenancy

By s.15(1) it is an implied term in *every assured periodic tenancy* that it may not be assigned nor sublet, nor may the tenant part with possession of it (in each case whether in whole or part) except with the consent of the landlords. Therefore, an unauthorised alienation will be a breach of the tenancy and give the landlord a discretionary ground for possession. Section 15(2) of the Act specifically provides that s.19 LTA 1927 does not apply to the term implied by s.15(1). The result is that, if s.15(1) applies, the landlord is free to withhold consent to the requests contemplated by s.15(1). Furthermore, the provisions of the Landlord and Tenant Act 1988 ('LTA 1988') do not apply where the statutory covenant is not qualified by the proviso that consent is not to be unreasonably withheld.

It should be noted that s.15(1) does *not* prohibit charging or mortgaging (whether in whole or part), nor does it prohibit parting with occupation whether of the whole or part. It follows that occupation whether of the whole or part, by e.g. a lodger to whom possession does not pass, would not be prohibited by sections 15(1) and 15(2).

It is possible, however, to override the terms implied by s.15(1). By s.15(3) where the assured tenancy in question is periodic (and *not* a statutory periodic tenancy) and is subject to one of the following terms namely:

(i) a provision (whether contained in the tenancy or not) which prohibits (either absolutely or conditionally) the assignment, subletting or parting with possession of the dwelling house; or
(ii) that a premium is required to be paid on the grant *or* renewal of the tenancy

then the implied term in s.15(1) is overridden and the terms of the tenancy in question apply. The expression 'premium' is defined in s.15(4) to 'include' any fine or like sum and any other pecuniary consideration in addition to rent. Premium also includes any sum paid by way of deposit which does not exceed one sixth of the *annual* rent payable under the tenancy immediately after the grant or renewal in question. The definition of premium is therefore not exclusive and is widely drawn. The expression 'any other pecuniary consideration' includes the payment of money or the foregoing of receipt of money: *Elmdene Estates* v. *White* [1960] AC 528.

It follows that if the tenancy is periodic the draftsman should include specific alienation provisions unless the provisions of s.15(1) are adequate. In assessing the potential impact of this section on a fixed term tenancy, consider that by s.5(2) where a fixed term tenancy comes to an end (otherwise than as mentioned in that section), then a periodic tenancy arises 'under which subject to the following provisions of this Part of this Act, the other terms are the same as those of the fixed term tenancy immediately before it came to an end'. Therefore it seems that a periodic tenancy which arises at the end of a fixed term tenancy by s.5(2) will be subject to the limitations on alienation set out in s.15(1).

(4) Access for repairs

By s.16 it is an implied term of every assured tenancy (whether fixed term or periodic) that the tenant shall afford the landlord access to the dwelling and all reasonable facilities for carrying out any repairs which the landlord is required to execute. In fact, for most assured tenancies the repair obligations are likely to fall on the landlord (see the discussion of s.116 of the Act at page 85 below) and such obligations will carry a right of entry, upon notice, insofar as this is necessary to execute repairs: *McGreal* v. *Wake* (1984) 13 HLR 107 CA.

(5) Succession

The Act does not concern itself with succession to a fixed term tenancy which is unexpired at the date of the death of the sole or sole surviving tenant. Such a tenancy will pass under the tenant's will or intestacy. Equally, the Act does not deal with a fixed term joint tenancy where one joint tenant dies, leaving a surviving joint tenant since the right of survivorship applies.

Section 17 relates to an assured periodic tenancy and grants a right of succession in respect of such a tenancy which is restricted to a single succession in favour of the spouse of a deceased sole tenant. In order to qualify, the tenant's spouse must have been occupying the dwelling-house immediately before the tenant's death as his or her only or principal home: s.17(1)(b). By s.17(4) 'spouse' includes a person living with the tenant 'as his or her wife or husband'. Therefore, both the actual and the common law spouse are capable of qualifying. In the case of a dispute as to the person entitled, the county court is required to decide the issue: s.17(5).

The spouse cannot, however, succeed to the tenancy if the deceased tenant was himself a 'successor' within s.17(2) or s.17(3), since the intention of the Act is to ensure that there can only be a single succession. A tenant is a successor to a tenancy within the meaning of s.17(2) if:

(a) the tenancy vested in him by virtue of s.17 or under the will or intestacy of a previous tenant: s.17(2)(a)
(b) the tenant was a sole survivor of a joint tenancy: s.17(2)(b)
(c) the tenant became entitled to the tenancy by survivorship under RA 1977 Part I Schedule I (for which see page 45 below): s.17(2)(c).

A tenant will also be a successor if he falls within the terms of s.17(3). This section contemplates that the deceased sole tenant had previously been a successor within the meaning of s.17(2) to a tenancy and had then been granted a new tenancy and that in each case the tenancy was of the same or substantially the same dwelling-house.

Assuming that the spouse is able to succeed to the tenancy on the death of the sole tenant, then the tenancy vests 'by virtue of' s.17 and does not devolve under the tenant's will or intestacy: s.17(1). For this reason ground 7 of Schedule 2 (which permits possession of the dwelling-house to be obtained within 12 months of the death of a tenant holding under a periodic tenancy) will not be available to the landlord since this ground only applies where the periodic tenancy 'has devolved under the will or intestacy of the former tenant'.

(6) Sub-tenancies and reversionary tenancies

Section 18(1) is intended to confer security of tenure on a sub-tenant whose immediate landlord's interest is determined by a superior landlord. Section 18(1) requires the sub-tenant to hold a lawful letting of a dwelling-house on an assured tenancy from a landlord who is himself a tenant (but not necessarily an assured tenant) under a superior tenancy. If the superior tenancy comes to an end, the sub-tenant becomes the direct tenant of the superior landlord. Section 18(1) will not however avail a sub-tenant whose 'new' (formerly superior) landlord falls within a class which cannot create an assured tenancy: see Schedule 1 paras 11 and 12.

Sub-sections 18(3) and (4) of the Act deal in a rather obscure fashion with reversionary tenancies and provide that such a tenancy will not, when it takes effect, defeat the rights of a tenant having an assured periodic tenancy. To this end it is provided that a reversionary tenancy granted so as to begin on or after either:

(a) the date upon which a statutory periodic tenancy came into being by reason of s.5(2); or
(b) a date on which a periodic tenancy could (in the absence of the Act) have been brought to an end by notice to quit

will take effect subject to the periodic tenancy in question.

(7) Restrictions on levy of distress for rent

By s.19(1) no distress for the rent of any dwelling-house let on an assured tenancy can be levied except with leave of the county court. The court has the same powers in relation to adjournment, stay, suspension, postponement etc. as are conferred on the county court under s.9 in respect of possession proceedings (see page 22 above).

However, under s.19(2) these restrictions do not apply to distress levied under s.102 County Courts Act 1984 ('CCA 1984') which permits goods to be seized in respect of sums owing in rent arrears where goods are also seized in execution of a county court judgment.

(8) Jurisdiction

Generally, by s.40 the county court has jurisdiction over questions arising in connection with both assured tenancies and assured shorthold tenancies other than a question falling within the jurisdiction of a rent assessment committee.

Chapter 4

Assured Shorthold Tenancies

4.01 Introduction

The majority of landlords seeking to create new assured tenancies after 15 January 1989 are likely to want to use the assured shorthold tenancy. The reason is that at the end of the term of the tenancy the landlord can obtain possession as of right. Furthermore, despite its name, the term of this form of tenancy need not be short; the Act requires that the tenancy be for a minimum term, not a maximum.

4.02 Definition

An assured shorthold tenancy is merely a form of assured tenancy (s.20(1)) so that an assured shorthold tenancy must satisfy the requirements of s.1 of the Act, and in addition:

(a) be for a fixed term certain (not periodic) of not less than six months: s.20(1)(a)
(b) contain no power for the landlord to determine the tenancy (except by forfeiture or re-entry for breach of any term or condition of the tenancy (s.45(4)) at any time earlier than six months from the beginning of the tenancy: s.20(1)(b)
(c) the prospective landlord must have served on the prospective tenant a notice in the prescribed form (see SI 1988 No. 2203, Form 7) before the tenancy is entered into stating that the assured tenancy is to be shorthold: s.20(1)(c), 20(2) and 20(6)(a).

Since s.20(1)(a) and (b) should be read together in the light of s.45(2) the minimum term prescribed will run from the day that the tenancy is entered into or (if later) the day on which the tenant is entitled to possession. Thus, for example, where a tenancy is created in mid term (e.g. a term created on 30 April to run from the previous 25 March) care must be taken to ensure that the fixed term will run for at least six months certain calculated from 30 April.

This may result in the term being longer than is required by the tenant. This need not prove a barrier since, whilst the landlord is not entitled to break the tenancy within six months from its beginning, there is no objection to the tenant having this option. Therefore a term certain of even six months which the tenant can break after (say) four months is valid.

Were it not for s.20(3) many landlords might be tempted to take advantage of the assured shorthold tenancy and persuade a tenant having an assured tenancy to take an assured shorthold tenancy, thus ensuring that the landlord could obtain possession in the future. By s.20(3) where a purported assured shorthold tenancy is granted, in circumstances where one or more of the tenants receiving the assured shorthold tenancy was, immediately before that grant, an assured (but not a shorthold) tenant and the landlord under both tenancies is the same, then the new tenancy cannot be shorthold.

The reference in s.20(3)(a) is to 'a tenant under an assured tenancy' so that the sub-section directs itself to the security previously enjoyed by the tenant and not to the dwelling-house which was the subject of that security. It is submitted, therefore, that a landlord who successfully persuades a tenant to move to a new dwelling-house will not avoid the consequences of s.20(3). However s.20(3)(b) imposes a requirement that the identity of the landlord must also remain the same. Thus a tenant who moves to new accommodation with a different landlord does not take his assured status with him.

Surprisingly there is a *quid pro quo* for s.20(3) contained in s.20(4). Where an assured shorthold tenancy comes to an end, and a new tenancy of the same or substantially the same premises arises between the same persons who were landlord or tenant of the expired assured shorthold, then the new tenancy will be an assured shorthold tenancy for so long as it remains assured: s.20(4). The provisions of s.20(4) apply even where the requirements of s.20(1)(a)–(c) are not met.

A landlord who does not wish a new assured shorthold tenancy to arise under s.20(4) can serve notice on the tenant to this effect. The only result will be to turn the shorthold tenancy into an assured tenancy. The notice must be served before either the new tenancy is entered into or the statutory periodic tenancy under s.5(2) takes effect in possession: s.20(5) and 20(6)(b).

4.03 *Recovery of possession of an assured shorthold tenancy*

(1) Introduction

The Act aims to make recovery of possession of an assured shorthold tenancy as simple as possible. The first question to decide is whether the assured shorthold tenancy is (or was granted for) a fixed term which has come to an end, or whether it is periodic.

(2) Fixed term assured shorthold tenancy

Where a fixed term assured shorthold tenancy has come to an end the landlord can obtain possession of it. All that is required is for the landlord to show that:

(i) he has given not less than two months' notice to the tenant stating that he requires possession;
(ii) the assured shorthold has come to an end; and
(iii) no further assured tenancy (other than a statutory periodic tenancy) has come into existence.

The notice may be given before or on the day on which the tenancy comes to an end: s.21(2). Therefore a landlord can give the notice immediately after the beginning of the tenancy. Where only a statutory periodic tenancy has come into being at the end of the fixed term, the statutory periodic tenancy terminates automatically on the day on which the possession order takes effect.

The reference to s.5(2) (statutory periodic tenancy) contains a trap for the unwary landlord who is tempted to negotiate fresh terms with his tenant before deciding to take possession proceedings; the statutory periodic tenancy will not arise under s.5(2) if the tenant can point to the 'grant of another tenancy' within the meaning of s.5(4). If such a grant has occurred, whilst the landlord may be saved from creating an assured (as opposed to a shorthold) tenancy by s.20(4), he may nevertheless be unable to obtain possession at the moment he desires to do so, and will have to start fresh possession proceedings.

(3) Periodic assured shorthold tenancy

The court is required to make an order for possession of a periodic assured shorthold tenancy where the landlord can show that notice has been served on the tenant stating that possession is required. The period specified in the notice cannot be less than two months (calculated from the date the notice is given). The notice must expire on a stated date being the last day of a period of the tenancy. In addition the stated date may not be earlier than the earliest date on which the periodic tenancy in question could be brought to an end at common law, by notice to quit given on the same day as the landlord served his notice under s.21(4)(a). Thus a periodic tenancy which is for a greater period than a month may take longer than two months to terminate. A quarterly tenancy, for example, would require a quarter's notice.

(4) Other methods of possession

A landlord can obtain possession of an assured shorthold tenancy on any of the grounds, and subject to the same procedures which apply to an equivalent assured tenancy: s.21(1) and s.21(4). However Chapter 1 of the Act clearly limits the court's powers in this respect so that it will be more normal to use the procedures laid down in s.21.

4.04   Rent

The rent under an assured shorthold is to be agreed by the parties and incorporated within the tenancy agreement. The landlord is given no statutory mechanism with which to increase the rent. However, whereas under s.13 the tenant cannot request a rent reduction by making a reference to the RAC, s.22 permits such a reference from an assured shorthold *tenant*.

The section states that this limited control exercisable by the RAC is over 'excessive' rent levels. A tenant of an assured shorthold tenancy can refer his rent to an RAC if he considers that the rent is significantly higher than the rents payable under similar shorthold tenancies in the locality. Subject to the exclusions considered below, the tenant can make this application at *any time* even on the day after the tenancy is entered into. The relevant form for a tenant's application is contained in SI 1988 No. 2203, Form 8 which is reproduced in Appendix III of this book.

Upon a tenant's application the RAC will determine the rent which in its opinion the landlord might reasonably be expected to obtain under the assured shorthold tenancy (c.f. s.78 RA 1977).

However, the RAC may only make such a determination if it considers that:

(i) There are a sufficient number of similar dwelling houses in the locality let on assured shorthold lettings.

It is the normal practice of RACs to work with 'comparables' – other similar properties for which a rent has already been fixed. In practice RACs are likely to have little difficulty with the notion of finding similar properties in the locality, although 'locality' is not defined. Under s.70(1) RA 1977, 'locality' was one factor which an RAC had to take into account in determining a fair rent. Case law permitted RACs to look across localities to find comparable areas in the absence of sufficient local comparables – see, e.g., *Meredith* v. *Stevens* (1974) 237 EG 573.

Given the restriction contained in s.22(3)(a) this is presumably no longer possible. There is, also, a catch 22 problem here. RACs cannot make determinations until there are sufficient assured shorthold tenancies locally. Yet until they begin to make determinations, they have few available comparators. It seems that initially RACs will be forced to investigate local letting conditions to build up their base of expert knowledge.

(ii) The rent payable under the tenancy in question is *significantly higher* than the rent which the landlord might reasonably expect to be able to obtain under the tenancy having regard to the levels of those other rents (s.22(3)). There is little guidance as to what might amount to a 'significantly higher' rent. Elsewhere landlord and tenant law has expended much energy debating what amounts to a 'substantial proportion' of the rent (see s.7 RA 1977 and s.43(1)(d) LTA 1954 and R.G. Lee and P. Luxton (1989) *Conv* p.59). In general the appellate courts are reluctant to disturb the findings of the RAC.

(iii) They have the necessary jurisdiction. The right of a tenant to refer a rent to the RAC arises only during the continuance of the original fixed term. Moreover it arises only once during that fixed term. Even if a second fixed term tenancy is granted, the tenant cannot invoke the s.22 procedure to refer the rent to the RAC. If a periodic tenancy arises, however, the landlord could refer under s.13 albeit he might have to wait until the first anniversary of the s.22 determination. As the tenant cannot make use of the s.13 procedure, it follows that the tenant of an assured shorthold of whatever length is permitted one opportunity to refer only.

If the RAC do make a determination under this provision it is to have effect from such date as the RAC directs, which may not be earlier than the date of the application (s.22(4)(a)). Any amount by which the contractual rent exceeds the determined rent is irrecoverable from the tenant (s.22(4)(b)). It should be noted that the RAC has no power to increase the rent.

While these are rather curious procedures it remains to be seen whether they are relied upon to any great extent by the tenant. Advisers to tenants will need to encourage the tenant to refer during the initial fixed term of tenancy, but will also wish to point to the absence of any security beyond the two months' notice which will provide the landlord with a ground upon which to recover possession. Experience in relation to restricted contracts shows that the vast majority of references to rent tribunals emanated from local authorities (under s.77 RA 1977) rather than from tenants, who were conscious of their lack of security. In the case of a tenant with a six month fixed term assured tenancy, even an early application to an RAC might lead to a determination to reduce the rent at a point which sees the end of the fixed term and a loss of effective security to the tenant.

Perhaps with a view to a potential reluctance to use these mechanisms, s.23 gives the Secretary of State a significant power by statutory instrument to remove the jurisdiction of RACs under s.22 absolutely or in certain areas or in other 'circumstances as may be specified in the order'.

Chapter 5

Other Forms of Letting

5.01 Transitional provisions

The Act represents an attempt to free the market from rent control. It seeks to do so by introducing the assured tenancy in place of Rent Act protected tenancies, and it follows that after 15 January 1989, the basic rule is that no protection under RA 1977 is available to new lettings. Existing tenancies subject to the Rent Acts remain, but even here there are transitional provisions to begin to unravel rent control (ss.34–39 of the Act). The adoption of the assured tenancy has necessitated arrangements for those few old assured tenancies under HA 1980 to be brought within the new regime. Certain transitional provisions relate also to housing association lettings.

(1) Protected tenancies and statutory tenancies under the Rent Act

Nothing in the Act affects the existing rights of Rent Act tenants. If a protected tenant's contractual tenancy is terminated after 15 January 1989, he holds over as a statutory tenant and the landlord can only regain possession under one of the cases set out in Schedule 15 of RA 1977.

However, under s.34(1) protected tenancies will essentially no longer be capable of coming into existence on or after the commencement of the Act. Protection will be given thereafter under the new regime. Section 34(1) states that a tenancy which is entered into on or after the commencement of the Act cannot be a protected or statutory tenancy, but goes on to outline four exceptional circumstances in which this may be possible:

(a) If it is entered into in pursuance of contract (e.g. an agreement for lease (see *Walsh* v. *Lonsdale* (1882) 21 ChD 9) made before 15 January 1989 (s.34(1)(a)).

(b) If it is granted to a person (alone or jointly with others) who, immediately before the tenancy was granted, was a protected or statutory tenant and the grant is made by the same landlord as under the protected or statutory tenancy (s.34(1)(b)). Note that the re-granted tenancy does not have to be of the same premises.

(c) Where an order for possession is made on the basis that suitable alternative accommodation was available (see s.98(1)(a) and Schedule 15 Part IV RA 1977) and a tenancy of that accommodation is then granted to a person (alone or jointly with others), then that tenancy may be a protected tenancy, providing the court directed that it should be so protected.

There are a number of points to note. Under the Act the availability of suitable alternative accommodation is a mandatory ground for possession (rather than a discretionary ground which it was under RA 1977). Consequently, if the court accepts that the accommodation is a suitable alternative it must order possession. However, if all that is offered to the tenant is the more limited protection of the assured tenancy it might be open to the tenant to defeat arguments that the accommodation – whatever its physical attributes – constitutes a suitable alternative (although the courts have been known to accept as suitable, leases which offered potentially less security: see *Edwards* v. *Cohen* (1958) 108 LJ News 556). For the law relating to the provision of suitable alternative accommodation, see R.E. Megarry *The Rent Acts*, 11th Edition at pp.443–59.

Legal advisers to protected or statutory tenants should seek to ensure that they obtain from the court a direction that the tenancy is granted as a protected tenancy.

(d) It is a tenancy under which, prior to 15 November 1990, a new town corporation transferred its landlord's interest to the private sector under s.38 of the Act (s.34(1)(d)) (see the note on 'Transfer from Public to Private Sector', at (6) below).

As regards rent, protected tenants will retain the right to apply for registration of a fair rent, during the lifetime of the contractual or statutory tenancy, and for re-registration of the rent at not less than two-yearly intervals. The ability of local authorities to refer a rent, on the tenant's behalf, to the rent officer under s.68 RA 1977 disappears, as does the right of a landlord (usually in advance of letting/ improvement of a dwelling) to apply for a certificate of fair rent under s.69 RA 1977.

(2) Protected shorthold tenancies

For a brief outline of protected shorthold tenancies see Chapter 2. Protected shorthold tenancies created before the commencement of the Act continue to be governed by HA 1980. However, new protected shorthold tenancies can only be created after 15 January 1989 in limited circumstances.

Of the possible circumstances for the creation of new protected tenancies outlined in the previous section (a–d), (d) (transfer of landlord's interest to the private sector) is unlikely to apply, and (b) (re-grant) is specifically excluded. Consequently it is possible to create a protected shorthold tenancy post-15 January 1989:

(a) in pursuance of a pre-15 January contract; or
(b) where the court direct that suitable alternative accommodation be provided in the form of a protected shorthold tenancy.

Note the importance of the exclusion of a re-grant of a tenancy. Where, on or after 15 January 1989, there is a renewal of a tenancy previously occupied on a protected shorthold, by the same landlord to the same tenant, then rather than a protected shorthold tenancy, the new tenancy will be deemed an assured shorthold tenancy.

This is so even though:

(i) At 15 January 1989 the tenancy was no longer a protected shorthold tenancy, it having expired and been allowed to continue with the tenant holding over as a protected tenant (see s.34(2)(b) and case 19 which, for the purpose of possession proceedings would include such tenancies within the term 'protected shorthold tenancies').
(ii) The necessary conditions for the creation of an assured shorthold tenancy (see s.20(1) and p.43 above) have not been met (s.34(3)).

However, it is possible for the landlord to prevent an assured shorthold tenancy arising by serving a s.20(5) notice (see above p.44) prior to the grant of a new tenancy. In most situations, the advantages will remain in permitting the continuance of an assured shorthold tenancy, but if the landlord felt, e.g., that there may be rental disadvantages in so doing, such a notice might be served. It would seem logical to allow the possibility of the s.20(5) notice to a landlord of a protected shorthold, but the Act is less than clear on the availability of such an option.

(3) Housing association lettings and licences

Briefly, s.35 provides for parallel provisions to protected tenancies (1(a)–(d) above) in relation to housing association lettings and licences. The fair rent scheme (RA 1977) and the secure tenancy scheme (HA 1985) will no longer apply except that there are saving provisions similar to those which apply to protected tenancies under RA 1977 (i.e. pre-commencement contract; regrant; suitable alternative accommodation; transfer of sector).

To these exceptions is added an additional one to cover occupiers who have purchased a dwelling designated as defective under Part XVI HA 1985. Such persons may demand that their former landlord repurchase the premises and re-let to them. Where this is done, even after 15 January 1989, the resulting tenancy will be a housing association (and not an assured) tenancy.

It should also be noted that there are further restrictions to the creation of secure tenancies in that the interest of the landlord must belong to specified bodies (s.35(4)). This includes, now, a housing action trust under Part III of the Act. All new housing association lettings created after 15 January 1989, apart from these exceptions, will be assured tenancies.

(4) Restricted contracts

Restricted contracts are defined under s.19(1) RA 1977 to include any tenancy or licence 'whereby one person grants to another person, in consideration of a rent which includes payment for the use of furniture or services, the right to occupy the dwelling as a residence'.

Existing rights under restricted contracts created prior to 15 January 1989 continue. This will lead to the gradual extinction of the restricted contract, but it will remain important to recognise those remaining for purposes of rent fixing (see Chapter 7), certain limited security depending on the date of the tenancy and protections from eviction.

Section 36(2) sets out the circumstances in which a variation of the terms of an existing restricted contract will take it outside RA 1977 protection. These are:

(a) if a variation affects the amount of the *rent* which, under the contract, is payable for the dwelling in question, then (subject to s.36(3)) the contract shall be treated as a new contract entered into at the time of the variation so that it is no longer a restricted contract for the purposes of the Act; and

(b) if the variation does not affect the amount of the rent payable under the contract but other terms of the agreement, then the question is simply whether such variations are so fundamental as to alter the nature of the letting – see e.g. *Welch* v. *Nagy* [1950] 1 KB 455. If so, then the contract will cease to enjoy Rent Act protection.

The above variations are deemed, in effect, to constitute a new letting. However, where a variation in rent results from either:

(a) rent-fixing by a rent tribunal, *or*
(b) an adjustment of rent in order to bring it into line with the registered rent

then no new contract may be assumed and the restricted contract continues.

Section 81A RA 1977 permits a landlord to apply for cancellation of a registered rent if two years have passed since the tribunal last fixed a rent and the premises are not, for the time being, subject to a restricted contract. Section 34(2) of the Act now withdraws the two year restriction, allowing the landlord to apply for cancellation whenever the dwelling ceases to be subject to a restricted contract.

(5) Existing assured tenancies under the Housing Act 1980

Assured tenancies under HA 1980 are considered in brief at p.4. Section (3) converts all such assured tenancies within s.56–58 HA 1980 under which the dwelling-house was let as a separate dwelling into assured tenancies under the Act, subject to certain very limited exceptions:

(a) where a landlord's interest belongs to the Crown or to a local authority (and the provisions of Schedule 1 paras 11 and 12 define this interest)
(b) where a tenant under an old-style assured tenancy has applied to the court for a new tenancy prior to 15 January 1989, the old tenancy will continue post 15 January as a 1980 Act tenancy. Once the court has made a determination, either the landlord will take possession if the application is refused, or if a new tenancy is granted, it will take the form of a new assured tenancy (assuming it does not fall within section (a) above).

Note that even where there is a contract for the grant of an old assured tenancy prior to 15 January 1989, it will take effect as a grant of a 1988 Act assured tenancy, in contrast to transitional arrangements elsewhere.

The provisions of the Act operate to convert 1980 assured tenancies whether or not they satisfy the requirements for assured tenancy status under the Act. In one respect this is particularly important. Fully mutual housing associations will not usually let premises on assured tenancies owing to restrictions in Schedule 1 para. 12(1)(h) of the Act. However, where the approved landlord of an old assured tenancy was a fully mutual housing association immediately prior to 15 January 1989, then the landlord, notwithstanding the tenancy, will become and remain an assured tenancy under the Act.

(6) Transfer from public to private sector

One of the aims of the Act is to promote the transfer of responsibility for residential lettings from the public to the private sector (see the tenants' choice provisions of Part IV of the Act and also ss.6–9 HPA 1986). Such a transfer implies a change in the status of the letting and s.38 regulates this.

The section provides that where the landlord's interest ceases to vest in a public body upon being transferred to a private landlord, the tenancy will become an assured tenancy under Part I of the Act. If, however, the reversion again vests in a public body the tenancy will reconvert into a secure tenancy. 'Public bodies' are defined in s.38(5).

In relation to housing association lettings, new tenancies will be assured (see page 52 above). However, existing housing association tenancies are secure tenancies under HA 1985, but on the housing association's interest being transferred to a private landlord the tenancy becomes an assured tenancy (s.38(2) and (3)). On the reversion revesting in the housing association, the tenancy becomes secure once again.

5.02   *Succession to statutory tenancies*

Under Schedule I of RA 1977 where a protected or statutory tenant died, a statutory succession to the tenancy was permissible. In certain circumstances, two such successions were possible. However, the Act introduces important amendments in the case of a tenant who dies after 15 January 1989. Except where the successor is the surviving spouse of the original tenant, the succeeding tenant will not be entitled to a statutory tenancy under RA 1977 but to an assured tenancy. Section 39 provides that s.2(1)(b) RA 1977 is to be amended in that an occupier who would otherwise take as statutory tenant by succession, rather than being entitled to a statutory tenancy, will be entitled to an assured tenancy by succession. Therefore s.2(1)(b) reads:

> 'Part 1 of Schedule 1 to this Act [i.e. RA 1977] shall have effect for determining what person (if any) is the statutory tenant of a dwelling-house *or, as the case may be, is entitled to an assured tenancy of a dwelling-house by succession* at any time after the death of a person who, immediately before his death, was either a protected tenant of the dwelling-house or the statutory tenant of it....'

Section 39(1) states that where the original tenant (which is defined in Part 1 of Schedule 1 RA 1977 as 'the person who, immediately before his death, was a protected tenant of the dwelling-house or the statutory tenant of it by virtue of his previous protected tenancy') dies after 15 January 1989, Part 1 of Schedule 1 RA 1977 shall have effect subject to the amendments in Part 1 of Schedule 4 of the Act. These amendments to the provisions under RA 1977 governing who is entitled to succeed the protected or statutory tenant are wide reaching.

(1) First succession

(i) *Original tenant dies after 15 January 1989 leaving a surviving spouse*

Paragraph 2 Part 1 Schedule 1 RA 1977 provided for the surviving spouse of the tenant to succeed the original tenant if residing in the dwelling-house immediately before the original tenant's death. The surviving spouse would then become the statutory tenant if and so long as the dwelling-house was occupied as his or her residence.

The Act largely keeps this structure in place. A surviving spouse of an original tenant still succeeds to a *statutory* tenancy under RA 1977 if and so long as the spouse continues to occupy the dwelling-house as a residence. Note that the surviving spouse has to have *resided* in the dwelling-house – whether or not he or she lived there with the deceased at the time of death.

The Act does, however, make one important change in the definition of spouse. For the purposes of the Rent Act 'spouse' does not include a co-habitee, although where a stable relationship existed, the courts have treated a co-habitee as a member of the family (e.g. *Dyson*

Holdings Ltd v. *Fox* [1976] QB 503). This has now been amended so that 'for the purposes of this paragraph, the person who was *living with* the original tenant as his or her wife or husband shall be treated as the spouse of the original tenant' (i.e. common law spouses are now protected): s.39(2). Note that the common law spouse has to be 'living with' the original tenant – not merely residing in the same property.

Under the Rent Acts, a claim to succeed by a spouse would take priority, but where no such claim could be substantiated, the co-habitee could claim as a 'member of the family'. As a result of the re-definition of the term 'spouse', provision has been made to cover the situation where there is more than one person claiming to be the 'spouse' entitled to the statutory tenancy by succession. In this situation the parties must either agree or in default of agreement the matter is referred to the county court.

(ii) Original tenant dies after 15 January 1989 leaving no surviving spouse but other members of his family

For a member of the original tenant's family to be entitled to succeed to the tenancy the person must have resided with the original tenant in the dwelling-house for a period of *two years* (rather than six months under RA 1977) *immediately* before the original tenant's death. The successor here will only be entitled to an *assured* tenancy. However, a claimant entitled to succeed on 15 January 1989 to the tenancy, having resided with the original tenant for six months under RA 1977, will not lose that right but will remain qualified so long as residence with the tenant continues. This is so even though the tenant may wish to succeed to a statutory tenancy before the two year requirement is met.

It should be noted that 'family' is not defined in the Act and existing case law will continue to apply. 'Family' is to be given its ordinary meaning. Lord Denning MR stated in *Dyson Holdings Ltd* v. *Fox* [1976] QB 503 that:

'It is not used in the sense in which it would be used by a studious and unworldly lawyer, but in the sense in which it would be used by a man who is "base, common and popular" to use Shakespeare's words in *Henry V* Act IV.'

It follows that 'family' includes more than blood relations. Russell LJ in *Ross* v. *Collins* [1964] 1 WLR 425 stated that 'family' included the situations:

'where the link would be strictly familiar had there been a marriage, or where the link is through the adoption of a minor, *de jure* or *de facto*, or where the link is "step-", or where the link is "in-law" or by marriage.'

Family does not include an artificial family link e.g. by two strangers calling themselves sisters (*Sefton Holdings Ltd* v. *Cairns* [1988] 1 EGLR 99) or aunt and nephew (*Carega Properties SA* v. *Sharratt* [1979] 1 WLR 928).
The phrase 'resided with' is also not defined – although some measure of community and family living must be shown (*Foreman* v. *Beagley* [1969] 1 WLR 1387). The successor has to show that he 'has become in a true sense part of the household' (*Swanbrae* v. *Elliott* [1987] 281 EG 916), and the question is one of fact and degree (*Chios Property Investment Co.* v. *Lopez* (1987) 20 HLR 120). The residence must be in the dwelling-house – not merely with the original tenant. A connection with the property is also, therefore, important.

(2) Second succession

The provisions as to who may succeed the 'first successor' have now been altered. Under RA 1977 the surviving spouse of the first successor would have been entitled to succeed if residing in the dwelling-house immediately before the death of the first successor, failing which a person who was a member of the first successor's family and was residing with him at the time of, and for a period of six months immediately before, his death would have been entitled to the statutory tenancy.
The following amendments made by the Act apply where the original tenant dies after 15 January 1989, or where the original tenant died before that date but his first successor dies after it.
The situation is now that, to be entitled to succeed, a person must be:

(i) a member of the *original* tenant's family *immediately* before the *tenant's death*, and
(ii) a member of the *first* successor's family *immediately* before the *first successor's death*, and
(iii) residing in the dwelling-house at the time of, and for the period of *two years* immediately before, the *first successor's death*. This second succession is to an *assured* tenancy. (It should be noted again that the two year requirement does not apply where the original tenant only lives for 18 months from 15 January 1989 – in that case the residency requirement is six months).

The second successor must be a member of *both* the original tenant's family and the first successor's family (in terms of the definition outlined above). This requirement narrows the scope for second successors, in an attempt to lead to a more rapid de-control of the market.

If there is more than one qualifying successor, such of them as may be decided by agreement or, in default of agreement, by the county court shall be entitled to an assured tenancy on the dwelling-house by succession.

It is important to realise that this second succession provision applies only where a statutory tenancy exists (i.e. where the first succession was by the spouse under s.39(2)). If the first succession is to an assured tenancy then there is no second succession either under s.39 or s.17.

(3) Summary and examples

Therefore, to summarise:

(i) A person living with the deceased protected or statutory tenant as a husband or wife will now be able to qualify as a surviving spouse and thus become a statutory tenant by succession if residing in the house immediately before the death of the deceased tenant.

Example:
Henry dies leaving a common law wife, Wendy. Wendy succeeds to a statutory tenancy if she was living with Henry immediately before his death.

(ii) If there is no qualifying 'surviving spouse' but a person who was a member of the original tenant's family residing in the dwelling-house with the tenant for a period of two years immediately before his death then that person will become entitled (not as before to a statutory tenancy by succession) but to an assured tenancy by succession.

Example:
Henry dies leaving no spouse but a daughter, Denise. Denise succeeds to an assured tenancy if she was living with Henry for two years immediately before his death.

(iii) A second succession to an assured tenancy will be possible by a person who was a member of the original tenant's family immediately before his death and was also a member of the first successor's family immediately before his death, providing he was living in the dwelling-house at the time of, and for two years immediately prior to, the first successor's death.

Example:
Henry dies leaving a spouse, Wendy and a son, Sidney. Wendy succeeds to a statutory tenancy as in (i) above. Wendy then dies. Sidney is then entitled to an assured tenancy if he was living with Wendy at the dwelling for two years prior to her death.

(4) Assured tenancies by succession

Section 39(5) states that where a person becomes entitled to an assured tenancy of the dwelling-house by succession that tenancy shall be a periodic tenancy. It will take effect in possession immediately after the death of the deceased tenant, and be deemed to have been granted to the successor by the landlord of the deceased tenant. The periods for the tenancy will match the rental periods of its forerunner, and on terms ascertained by s.39(6), subject to the possibility of variation using the s.6 procedure.

Under s.39(7), if, immediately before the death of the predecessor, the landlord could have recovered possession under case 19 of Schedule 15 RA 1977 (i.e.) a mandatory ground for possession of a protected shorthold tenancy), the assured periodic tenancy to which the successor becomes entitled shall be an assured shorthold tenancy, whether or not it fulfils the conditions in s.20(1) HA 1988 (see pp. 43 above). This is mostly intended to apply where the deceased tenant was holding over following the expiry of a fixed term shorthold, but where case 19 can apply nonetheless.

Section 39(9) provides that, where, immediately before his death, the predecessor was a tenant under a fixed term tenancy, s.6 (which applies to statutory periodic tenancies) shall apply in relation to the assured periodic tenancy to which the successor becomes entitled on a predecessor's death.

Where a landlord served RA 1977 notices on an original tenant to preserve his rights to regain possession, any notices given in relation to cases 13–15 in Schedule 5 RA 1977 shall be treated, in relation to the new assured tenancy, as given for whichever of the grounds 3–5 in Schedule 2 of the Act corresponds with the case in question (s.39(10) and para. 15 of Schedule 4).

Similarly s.39(10) and para. 13 of Schedule 4 extend the application of cases 11, 12, 16–18 and 20 to an assured tenancy by succession, where the original tenancy was governed by RA 1977.

Chapter 6

Protection from Eviction

In many cases under the new regime, the landlord will have a great incentive to recover possession of the premises from existing protected tenants in order to re-let under the new provisions, and take advantage of the higher rental levels. Moreover the experience of decontrol under the Housing Act 1957 has shown that landlords may wish to take the opportunity to repossess in order to sell, depending upon the state of the housing market. In a freer market, this should be an option open to the landlord, but equally, there need to exist certain tenant protections to ensure that landlords do not seek to evict by illegal means, or without due process of law. In order to ensure this, the Act takes the opportunity to amend and extend the Protection from Eviction Act 1977 ('PFEA 1977'). There are three broad strategies pursued in order to protect tenants from unlawful eviction: recourse to the criminal law, extension of civil liability and procedural safeguards.

6.01 Criminal liability

(1) Introduction

Under PFEA 1977, there are two broad offences in relation to eviction. The first of these, to be found in s.1(2), governs unlawful eviction, and is unamended by the Act. It protects residential occupiers – persons occupying premises as a residence – and is broad enough to cover rights to occupy under contract, statute or other rule of law. Where any person attempts to deprive, or succeeds in depriving, such an occupier of his occupation of the premises, by unlawful means, that person is guilty of an offence of unlawful eviction.

Alongside this offence exists the offence of unlawful harassment (see s.1(3)). Section 29 has introduced amendments. The section now states that any person who does an act likely (previously 'calculated') to interfere with the peace or comfort of the residential occupier or

members of his household, or who persistently withdraws or withholds services reasonably required for the occupation of the premises
as a residence, commits the offence of unlawful harassment. The Act
has replaced the word 'calculated' by the word 'likely', but this does not
seem to have any substantive effect on the *actus reus* of the offence. The
defendant must intend to cause the residential occupier to give up
occupation permanently (*Schon* v. *Camden LBC* [1986] 2 EGLR 37 and *R*
v. *Yuthiwattana* (1984) 16 HLR 49) or at least to refrain from exercising
any right or remedy in respect of the premises.

(2) New offence of harassment

However, the more significant amendment to PFEA 1977 is the
introduction of a new offence of harassment (a new s.1(3A)).

Harassment will henceforth be committed where any person does
acts which are '*likely*' (*not* 'calculated' as under PFEA 1977) to interfere
with the peace and comfort of the residential occupier or members of
his household (s.29(1)). This will probably be easier to prove than the
PFEA 1977 wording. Section 29(2) introduces this new offence of
harassment into PFEA 1977, the new s.1(3A), which can only be
committed by a landlord (including a superior landlord) or his agent
(not any person) who:

(i) does acts likely to interfere with the peace or comfort of the
residential occupier or members of his household, or
(ii) persistently withdraws or withholds services reasonably
required for the occupation of the premises in question as a
residence

and (in either case) knows, or has reasonable cause to believe, that the
conduct is likely to cause the residential occupier to give up the
occupation of the whole or part of the premises or to refrain from
exercising any right, or pursuing any remedy, in respect of the whole
or part of the premises.

However, a person is not guilty of an offence under s.1(3A) if he
proves that he had reasonable grounds for doing the acts or
withdrawing or withholding the services in question. Mistake as to the
extent of those legal rights is not a defence, but a mistake made on
reasonable grounds that the persons subject to the landlord's actions
were not residential occupiers may be (see *R*. v. *Phekoo* [1981] 1 WLR
1117).

The main difference between the two offences of harassment

relates to *mens rea*. Under the previous law it had to be proved that the defendant acted 'with intent to cause'. Under the new offence it is sufficient if actual knowledge or a reasonable cause to believe is proved. This should make it easier to obtain convictions. Maximum penalties are the same for all three of the offences above: on summary conviction, a fine at the prescribed amount (maximum £2000) and/or six months' imprisonment; on indictment, an unlimited fine and/or two years' imprisonment.

6.02   Civil liability

(1) Introduction

Existing remedies for unlawful eviction and harassment remain unchanged by the Act. First the occupier may seek injunctive relief, perhaps accompanied by damages. Such damages may be based upon breach of contract (usually the breach of the implied covenant for quiet enjoyment) or in tort (for trespass to person or property). Classic examples of unlawful eviction and harassment include cutting off gas and electricity supplies, removing the occupier's personal belongings from the premises and intimidatory behaviour.

(2) New tort of unlawful eviction

Section 27 of the Act creates a new tort allowing the occupier to recover damages from a landlord who personally or through agents has committed acts which amount to the offences under sI of PFEA 1977 (c.f. *McCall* v. *Abelesz* [1976] QB 585 disallowing this possibility).

Basis of liability
Section 27(2) provides that damages for unlawful eviction are available if a landlord (in this section referred to as 'the landlord in default') or any person acting on behalf of the landlord in default:

(i)   attempts unlawfully to deprive the residential occupier of any premises of his occupation of the whole or part of the premises, or

(ii) knowing or having reasonable cause to believe that the conduct is likely to cause the residential occupier of any premises

(a) to give up his occupation of the premises or any part thereof, or

(b) to refrain from exercising any right or pursuing any remedy in respect of the premises or any part thereof,

does acts likely to interfere with the peace or comfort of the residential occupier or members of his household, or persistently withdraws or withholds services reasonably required for the occupation of the premises as a residence, and, as a result, the residential occupier gives up his occupation of the premises as a residence.

This liability is imposed in relation to acts occurring after 9 June 1988 and arises irrespective of whether there has been a conviction for the offence (but where such a conviction exists it can be used as evidence in the civil proceedings). Although, in order to satisfy the requirements of s.27 in relation to liability for damages, the defendant need not have succeeded in evicting the occupier, the occupier must have been caused to give up his occupation of 'the demised premises' (not a *part* of the premises).

The liability is tortious and additional to any other liability in damages (e.g. breach of quiet enjoyment or trespass). The tort rules on remoteness will apply and it may be possible to award exemplary damages. In *Drane* v. *Evangelou* [1978] 1 WLR 455, £1000 was awarded for 'monstrous' behaviour. Because s.27(5) states that the plaintiff should not be compensated twice for the same loss, it remains to be seen whether the courts will restrict the award of punitive damages where the new remedy is invoked. One suspects that the growth of exemplary damages reflected the absence of a remedy for unlawful eviction *per se*.

It should also be remembered that the standard of proof in civil cases is based on the balance of probabilities – a lower standard than for criminal cases.

(3) Defences and mitigation

Section 27(6) provides that there will be no liability if, by the date on which the proceedings to enforce liability are finally disposed of, the residential occupier has been reinstated (whether by the landlord or court order) on the premises in question. It would therefore appear sensible that, if the residential occupier has taken alternative accommodation, the landlord should ensure the occupier positively agrees to forego or abandon any claim under s.27(3).

Note that an occupier does not have to accept an offer of reinstatement, but where such an offer takes effect in advance of the commencement of proceedings, then the damages available to the occupier may be reduced insofar as the court considers the refusal to be unreasonable: see s.27(7)(b). It may be open to the occupier to argue that the refusal is not unreasonable in view of the defendant's past behaviour. However, a better course is for the occupier to commence proceedings immediately, as thereafter refusals of offers to reinstate cannot lead to a reduction of awards of damages. As we shall see, the available award of damages may be such that it will become less likely for tenants, in a position to do so, to seek reinstatement.

It should also be noted that an occupier is under a duty to take reasonable steps to mitigate his loss (s.27(7)(a))

A defendant is offered a defence to the proceedings if he can prove that he believed, or had reasonable cause to believe, either that (i) the occupier had ceased to reside in the premises or (ii) he, the landlord, had reasonable grounds for withdrawing or withholding services (where the occupier claims that the landlord is liable because of such a withdrawal or withholding).

(4) Damages

Section 28(1) provides that the basis for the assessment of damages referred to in s.27(3) is the difference in value, determined as at the time immediately before the residential occupier ceased to occupy the premises in question as his residence, between:

(a) the value of the interest of the landlord in default determined on the assumption that the residential occupier continues to have the same right to occupy the premises as before that time, and

(b) the value of that interest determined on the assumption that the residential occupier has ceased to have that right

(i.e. the difference between the value of the premises tenanted and with vacant possession).

It is the landlord's interest in the *building* in which the premises are situated, not just his interest in the demised premises, which has to be valued (s.28(2)). Thus a tenant who is the sole remaining Rent Act protected occupier of a part of a much larger building may recover extensive damages. It follows also that the valuation will greatly depend on the legal security of the occupier – the greater the tenant's security, the higher the damages.

Section 28(3) provides that for the purposes of valuation it should be assumed:

(a) that the landlord in default is selling his interest on an open market basis to a willing buyer;

(b) that neither the residential occupier nor any member of his family wishes to buy; and

(c) any substantial development of the building or its site is unlawful, as is the demolition of the whole or part of any building on the land.

Some elaboration of this final point is necessary in order to explain the word 'substantial'. Any development which could be permitted by the Town and Country Planning General Development Order 1988 (SI 1988 No. 1813) will not be considered substantial; nor, where the dwelling is a flat within a larger building, will a change of use to residential use for the whole or part of the building.

Any other development will be considered substantial and a valuation based on this possibility must be disallowed. However, legal advisers to plaintiff tenants in a s.27 claim should request valuations from surveyors which take account of the possibility of permitted developments outlined above.

(5) County court jurisdiction

It is also important to consider s.40 of the Act in relation to damages awarded under the PFEA 1977. Section 40 (1) provides that the county court has jurisdiction under ss.27 and 28 (but excluding questions falling within the jurisdiction of a Rent Assessment Committee).

An important proviso is contained in s.40(2) to the effect that damages claimed in any proceedings under s.40(1) may exceed the amount which is the county court limit under the County Court Act 1984.

Under s.40(3), the county court has jurisdiction to hear and determine any other proceedings joined with proceedings under s.40(1). This is notwithstanding the fact that these additional proceedings would otherwise be outside the county court's jurisdiction (and therefore include proceedings which would otherwise be within the jurisdiction of the RAC).

Section 40(4) provides that if a person takes proceedings under s.40(1) in the High Court, he would only be able to recover costs on the county court scale. Thus, it is always important to take proceedings in the county court. Note, however, s.40(5) which allows proceedings to be taken in the High Court without any costs penalty where the proceedings were to enable them to be joined with any proceedings already pending before that court, or which were outside the ambit of s.40(1).

6.03   *Procedural safeguards*

(1) Eviction

Section 3 of PFEA 1977 restricts the ability of a landlord to regain possession of the premises without a court order in certain situations. Prior to 1989, the section applied where premises were let under a tenancy which was not a statutorily protected tenancy, and that tenancy had come to an end, but with the occupier continuing to reside in the whole or part of the premises. In such circumstances a breach of the prohibition is not of itself an offence (although in practice it will commonly amount to the offence of unlawful eviction) but the statutory prohibition gives rise to the availability of an injunction to restrain eviction or restore possession to an occupier unlawfully evicted.

Section 30 of the Act does not amend the offence of unlawful eviction but it amends s.3 PFEA 1977 so as to alter the circumstances in which an eviction without court proceedings is lawful.

Under PFEA 1977 only licensees with a restricted contract (entered into post-1980) fell within the ambit of s.3 and could be removed only after court proceedings. Other licensees could be removed from the premises without court proceedings provided that the contract had been properly terminated (if not, the licensor would be guilty of the offence of unlawful eviction under s.1 PFEA 1977 which extends to licences). The new s.3(2B), introduced by s.30(2) of the Act, extends s.3 to licences relating to a dwelling entered into on or after 15 January 1989.

(2) Excluded tenancies and licences

However, having widened the ambit of s.3, the Act curtails its full application. As before, it will not extend to tenancies protected already by the Rent Acts. In addition, s.31 of the Act adds a group of excluded tenancies and licences in respect of which it will be unnecessary to institute court proceedings for possession. It should be remembered that these excluded tenancies and licences must be properly terminated in accordance with their own terms, and any repossession must not include a use or threat of violence under the criminal law (see, for example, s.6, Criminal Law Act 1977).

The new s.3A lists the following excluded tenancies and licences:

(i) Those under which accommodation is shared with either the landlord or with a member of the landlord's family (see the definition in s.113 HA 1985 which applies), whether or not it is shared with others. It is provided that, for these purposes, shared accommodation does *not* include a storage area, staircase, passage, corridor or other means of access, but it will include living rooms, kitchens and bathrooms.

Both immediately before the tenancy/licence was granted and also at the time it comes to an end, the landlord must occupy the premises of which the whole or part of the shared accommodation formed a part as his only or principal home. These conditions must be fulfilled in the case of a member of the landlord's family sharing accommodation. Here, however, there is an additional requirement that the landlord also occupies premises, of which the whole or part of the shared accommodation formed a part, as his only or principal home, immediately before grant, and upon termination, of the tenancy/licence.

Check carefully the status of your resident landlord before advising upon the necessity of a court order. Non-sharing landlords are not excluded from the application of s.3 of the 1977 Act.

(ii) Those granted as a temporary expedient to a person who originally entered the premises as a trespasser, whether the tenancy or licence is the first granted or a later one. In the case of later grants these must take the form of temporary expedients.

(iii) Those relating to holiday lettings (see the earlier discussion relating to assured tenancy status and para. 9 Schedule 1 which contains an identical definition: see p.14 above).

(iv) Those granted gratuitously - i.e. other than for money or money's worth.

(v) Licences of hostel accommodation provided by a designated body (to which list the Secretary of State can add - see s.3A(8) and (9) PFEA 1977 and, for the definition of hostels applicable here, see s.622 HA 1985).

The landlord's ability to regain possession without a court order may make it more difficult for a tenant to argue that a particular arrangement (e.g. holiday letting) is a sham, and therefore within legislative protection rather than outside it, as such argument might be made most easily if the landlord faced the necessity of a court order. In the excluded cases the landlord would not need a court order to enforce his right to possession and the tenant would himself have to initiate proceedings, presumably by seeking a declaration or injunction.

(3) Notices to quit

Section 5 PFEA 1977 sets out various requirements for notices to quit – i.e. they must contain statutorily prescribed information and allow a minimum period of four weeks' notice (prescribed form SI 1988 No. 2201). Section 32 of the Act extends these provisions to periodic licences of residential property, but not to excluded tenancies or licences. (The same excluded tenancies or licences as considered early in this chapter at paras 2(i)–(v).)

Therefore, the rights of some occupiers (notably tenants who share accommodation with their landlord) have been significantly curtailed since they are no longer entitled either to a minimum of four weeks' notice or to be evicted only following court proceedings. However, these new rules only apply to tenancies entered into on or after 15 January 1989. It should also be remembered that tenancy agreements must be terminated in accordance with their own terms to prevent an offence under s.I. PFEA 1977 being committed.

Chapter 7

The Role of the Rent Assessment Committee and Rent Officers

It will be clear from the earlier consideration of rents for assured and assured shorthold tenancies, that the rent fixing functions under Part 1 of the Act devolve entirely upon the RAC. The two-tier process for fair rents under the RA 1977, whereby the initial determination is made by the rent officer, with the possibility of appeal to an RAC, continues. Under the assured tenancy regime, however, the RAC is charged with sole responsibility for matters in relation to rent. The role of the rent officer in relation to housing benefit assessments is considered below.

7.01 Rent assessment committees

(1) Constitution of rent assessment committees

The RAC is drawn from a panel of members (Rent Assessment Panel) which consists of persons appointed by the Secretary of State for the Environment (in England). There are 13 areas containing panels within England, with separate arrangements for Scotland and Wales. In practice they consist of lawyers, valuers and lay members. In general the lawyer acts as chairman, but this function can be fulfilled by a valuer-member, providing that the person chairing the committee has been appointed by the Lord Chancellor. Supervision of the work of RACs is by the Council on Tribunals under the Tribunal and Inquiries Act 1971 ('TIA 1971') Schedule 1 Part 1.

In practice, the day-to-day running of RACs is undertaken by the president of the panel alongside one or more persons acting as vice-presidents. Such persons are nominated by the Secretary of State and appointed by the Lord Chancellor. The president has an available staff of clerks and other officers to serve the various RAC's ranks. These members of staff are civil servants, and the remuneration and allowances available to panel members are provided directly by central government, unlike rent officers whose appointment, supervision and payment is the responsibility of the appropriate local authority (as to the status of a rent officer see *Department of the Environment* v. *Fox* [1980] 1 All ER 58).

(2) New functions of rent assessment committees

RACs have been given three separate functions under Part 1 of the Act. These are discussed more fully in earlier parts of this work. They consist of:

  (i) determining the terms of statutory periodic tenancies where new terms are proposed under s.6
 (ii) determining the level of any increase in rent for a statutory periodic tenancy or other contractual assured periodic tenancy where an application has been made by the landlord under s.13
(iii) determining any rent reduction to the level of a market rent for an assured shorthold tenancy where the tenant has made the claim under s.22 that the rent payable is excessive insofar as it exceeds the market level.

(3) Rent assessment committee procedure

The procedure which the RAC should observe in performing its functions is prescribed in the Rent Assessment Committee (England and Wales) Regulations 1971, SI 1971 No. 1065. These regulations have been amended (see SI 1980 No. 1699 and 1981 No. 1783) in order to extend the functions of RACs. By a further statutory instrument (SI 1988 No. 2200) the 1971 regulations now cover references made under the Act in order to fulfil the functions outlined in the previous paragraph (ss.6, 13 or 22 of the Act).

When an application is received under the Act by the RAC the initial question will be that of jurisdiction. For example, the timing of a reference under all three of the relevant sections of the 1988 Act may be fatal to the jurisdiction of the RAC. If it appears to the RAC that the application does not fall within its jurisdiction, then it will dismiss the reference, indicating why it is felt that the reference is invalid. Such decisions are subject to judicial review (see below).

The committee will then have to ascertain whether it is in possession of such information as is 'reasonably' required to enable it to carry out its function. If not, then it can request further information by serving upon either landlord or tenant a notice under s.41(2) of the

Act. The content of this form is prescribed by SI 1988 No. 2203 (Form 9) and is reproduced in Appendix III of this book. This form requires the party on whom it is served to give the committee within a period of not less than 14 days from service such information as the RAC may reasonably require for the purpose of its functions, as set out on the form.

A party who fails without reasonable excuse to comply with a notice served commits a criminal offence, and may be liable on summary conviction to a fine not exceeding level 3 on the standard scale (currently £400). Note that the local authority, rather than the RAC, is the prosecution agency in cases of breach of the s.41(3) provision (see s.222 of the Local Government Act 1972). In practice, the clerk to the RAC may seek information by simply corresponding with the parties.

(4) Hearings and representations

The amended regulations make provisions similar to those in Schedule 11 para. 7(1)(b) RA 1977 allowing the RAC to serve notice on landlord and tenant specifying a period during which representations in writing, or a request to make oral representations, may be made to the committee. The RAC must allow at least seven days from the service of the notice, although, in practice, panels usually allow a longer period – often 14 days – under the Schedule 11, RA 1977 powers. As the regulations stand, a party is given the choice of either written representations or a hearing, but does not seem to be able to opt for both.

Where either party makes a request for oral representation within the specified period, the RAC must allow the hearing. Such a hearing will invariably be public, although the committee has the discretion to decide otherwise. It is the practice of the RAC to arrange a hearing in the locality of the dwelling. In general, at least ten days' notice will be given of the date, time and place of the hearing, and where that time is altered, a further ten days should be allowed (see *R* v *Devon and Cornwall Rent Tribunal ex parte West* (1974) 20 P & CR 316).

The regulations specifically provide for legal representation where that is desired by either party. RACs are not bound by strict rules of evidence (c.f. *R.* v *Paddington North and St Marylebone Rent Tribunal ex parte Perry* [1956] 1 QB 229) but where either oral or documentary evidence is admitted, both parties must have the opportunity to comment upon it. It may be, however, that in its deliberations the RAC uses its own knowledge and experience. This is perfectly permissible, and evidence introduced in this way does not necessitate consultation with the parties (see *Crofton Investment Trust Ltd* v. *Greater London RAC* [1967] 2 QB 955).

(5) Inspections

The RAC can decide whether or not to inspect the premises in question. However, if it is specifically requested to do so by one or both parties, an inspection must be undertaken. Under the new regime, it may be more necessary than before for the RAC to inspect. It is not acting as an appellate body from the Rent Officer in discharging its functions in relation to assured tenancies, and the ambit of those functions under s.6 is wider than before. However, the RAC has no statutory right of entry, and its practice if entry is refused is generally to attempt to fix a further date for inspection.

If the RAC is yet again unsuccessful in gaining access, it would generally proceed to determine the rent on the evidence available to it, and indeed is under a duty to use whatever evidence it can gather (e.g. on external inspection) together with its knowledge and experience in order to discharge its functions (see *Daejan Properties Ltd* v. *Chambers* [1986] 1 EGLR 167).

There is no consistent pattern amongst panels as to whether to inspect before or after the hearing. It is, however, important to keep inspection separate from the hearing, and not to hear evidence from one party on inspection which is not considered at the hearing (under the principles laid down by the House of Lords in *Fairmount Investments Ltd* v. *Secretary of State for the Environment* [1976] 1 WLR 1255).

Because in the past the RACs have dealt with issues in relation to fair rents on appeal from the rent officer, the RAC usually had available inventories and measurements on the file. Whilst it would check this, the presence of this material generally made the work of the RAC easier and speedier. Inspections which relate to the functions exercised under the assured tenancy regime are likely to involve more work, particularly for the valuer-member. However, RACs will have some experience in fulfilling these tasks, since they will be akin to that discharged by Rent Tribunals in relation to restricted contracts. In practice, since the passage of s.72 HA 1980, the functions of Rent Tribunals have been exercised by RACs, so that it is wrong to regard members of the Rent Assessment Panel as only ever having discharged an appellate function.

(6) Comparables

According to *Mason* v. *Skilling* [1974] 1 WLR 1437 the factors to be considered in valuation are themselves part of the professional skill and experience of the RAC. It follows from this that RACs are free to look towards rents which they have fixed in the past on comparable properties. In order to fulfil their functions under ss.14 and 22, it seems apparent that RACs will have to use comparables. However, as no artificial considerations as to scarcity apply (c.f. s.70(2) RA 1977) there seems little reason why only registered comparables should be used by RACs, and landlord and tenant ought to be free to place before the RAC whatever evidence they can muster as to appropriate market rents in the locality. The RAC will remain free, nonetheless, to place greater reliance on their own knowledge (see *Crofton Investments Trust* v. *Greater London RAC* [1967] 2 QB 955).

Because references under Part 1 of the Act will take at least a year in most cases, much of the workload of the RAC under the Act will not be immediate. In the knowledge of this RACs have been gathering evidence as to market rents by what is known as a 'beacon' exercise – an investigatory process whereby panel members have attempted to monitor current market rents. This process will be assisted by liaison with Chief Rent Officers in order to compare evidence as to market levels. This has been rendered necessary by the elimination of the role of the rent officer in fixing rents under the Act (as to which, see below).

(7) Decisions

The decision of an RAC is recorded in documents signed by the chairman and forwarded to both parties. If requested (on or before the notification of the decision) to state reasons for that decision, the RAC must do so. In 1981, by virtue of Regulation 1981 No. 1783, the necessity for the RAC to give reasons in all cases was removed. Consequently unless written reasons are requested, these will not generally be provided by the RAC.

There has been an acceptance by the courts that the amount of reasoning which can be given in support of a valuation is limited (see for example *Guppys (Bridport) Ltd* v. *Sandoe* (1975) 30 P & CR 69, 75). On the other hand it is good practice for RACs to outline the comparables which they have used and to give reasons for accepting some comparables and rejecting others (see *Waddington* v. *Surrey and Sussex RAC* (1982) 264 EG 717 and *R.* v. *London Rent Assessment Committee ex parte St George's Court Ltd (No.1)* (1983) 265 EG 984). The Court of Session has consistently placed a higher standard in relation to RAC reasons on fair rent in Scotland, demanding a more detailed explanation of the determination reached (see *Albyn Properties Ltd* v. *Knox* [1977] SC 108).

It is arguable that a failure to give reasons is not of itself a ground upon which to set the decision aside, but it may lead to a court inferring that relevant factors have not been taken into account so as to enable them to do so (see *R* v. *London Rent Assessment Committee's ex parte St George's Court Ltd (No.1) (supra)*). Alternatively, the court might simply remit the matter to the RAC for reconsideration.

(8) Withdrawal

In relation to the functions of RACs under the Act, the ability of the parties to withdraw a reference at any point in the process has been considered in the main body of this work. It is perhaps necessary to emphasise that a withdrawal should be by both parties in writing. Similarly an RAC is not required to proceed to a determination if the tenancy has come to an end (see ss.6(8), 14(8), and 22(5)).

(9) Appeals

Although the Act does not lay down any provision for appeal, under s.13(1) TIA 1971 appeal on a point of law lies to the High Court. Indeed under this Act there is also the power to seek the opinion of the court by case stated, in which case the RAC will adjourn pending the outcome (see s.13(2) and *Trustees of Henry Smith's Charity* v. *Hemmings* (1981) 45 P & CR 377 (later affirmed in the Court of Appeal)). The procedures for appeals are governed by RSC Orders 55, 56 and 94.

An error of law may also give rise to an application for judicial review, as will any breach of the requirements of natural justice (see for example *Metropolitan Properties* v. *Lannon* [1968] 3 WLR 694). Legal advisers will need to consider carefully the merits of the appeal and judicial review procedures. Under RSC Order 53 leave is required prior to judicial review, but notwithstanding this, the advantages of this process (as outlined in *Ellis and Sons Fourth Amalgamated Properties Ltd* v. *Southern Rent Assessment Panel* (1984) 14 HLR 48) have allowed the judicial review procedure to emerge as the favourite method of challenging RACs. Judicial review, although not confined to matters of jurisdiction or breaches of natural justice, will not always be available, but fortunately the courts seem to adopt a flexible attitude in handling cases which may technically be brought under the wrong procedure (see *Lannon (supra)*).

(10) Recording of rents

Section 42(1) of the Act permits the Secretary of State to require the president of every RAC to keep and make publicly available such information as may be specified with respect to rents under assured tenancies which have been the subject of references or applications to, or determinations by, RACs. This the Secretary of State has now done under the Assured Tenancies and Agricultural Occupancies (Rent Information) Order 1988 (SI 1988 No. 2199). That Order applies to determinations made under ss.13 and 22 of the Act. It also includes those cases in which the RAC is precluded from making a determination under s.22(1) by virtue of s.22(3) of the Act. This is intended, presumably, to cover cases in which the RAC finds that a rent is not significantly higher than that which the landlord might reasonably be expected to be able to obtain under an assured shorthold tenancy.

The president of each panel will keep the information available for public inspection without charge during normal office hours, or provide a copy of the relevant information upon payment of a fee of £1 for the specified information relating to each determination. The specified information is as follows:

(i) address of premises

(ii) description of premises

(iii) names and addresses of landlord and tenant

(iv) if granted for a term, date of commencement of the tenancy and length of term

(v) the rental period

(vi) allocation between landlord and tenant of liabilities for repairs

(vii) whether any rates are borne by the landlord or a superior landlord

(viii) details of services provided by the landlord or a superior landlord

(ix) details of furniture provided by the landlord or a superior landlord

(x) any other terms of the tenancy or notice relating to the tenancy taken into consideration in determining the rent

(xi) the rent determined, the date it was determined and the amount (if any) of the rent which, in the opinion of the committee, is fairly attributable to the provision of services, except where that amount is in their opinion negligible, or, in a case where the committee is precluded from making a determination by s.22(3) of Act, the rent currently payable under the assured shorthold tenancy.

(11) Conclusion

In conclusion the workload of RACs under the Act can be predicted as follows:

(i) In relation to their functions as Rent Tribunals (see s.72 HA 1980) it may be expected that this workload will diminish, following the repeal of the ability of local authorities to make references under s.77 RA 1977.

(ii) In relation to the fair rent provisions of RA 1977, these functions will continue, but gradually dwindle over a long period of years as the number of Rent Act protected tenancies begins to decline.

(iii) As regards work under Part 1 of the Act, this may begin slowly with a few tenant references for assured shorthold tenancies under s.22.

(iv) Referrals under ss.6 and 13 will take longer to arrive, but then are likely to provide the bulk of the RAC work in the longer term. However, the level of this work will depend upon the ability of the landlord to reach agreement with the tenant without the necessity of referring the matter to the RAC. Moreover, the overall workload will be determined by the success of the legislation in promoting the growth of the private rented sector.

7.02   *The changing role of rent officers*

(1) Rent fixing

As the new forms of letting become commonplace, the traditional role of rent officers in relation to fixing fair rents under the Rent Acts will diminish. While the rent officer will continue to exercise this function in relation to existing premises protected by the Rent Acts, the RAC will enjoy the sole responsibility fo. the determination of rents for assured tenancies. This being the case, s.20 and Schedule 14 amend the enabling provisions of RA 1977 in relation to the Secretary of State's role in administering the scheme of rent registration. The changes will permit the reorganisation of the rent officer service, in particular by empowering the Secretary of State to amalgamate the rent officer's services across registration areas. There will be no new appointment of deputy rent officers, although the new scheme of appointment will allow for the designation of chief and senior rent officer. Finally, schedule 14 permits the appointment of rent officers for a fixed term.

All of these powers envisage a gradual running down of the work of the rent officer service, and may eventually lead to the shift away from the rent officer's traditional alignment to the local authority. A new s.64B is written into RA 1977, allowing the withdrawal of the powers of appointment, remuneration and administration of rent officers from local authority control. This power may be exercised in relation to local authorities generally or a particular local authority. Upon its exercise, the Secretary of State is given the power to make such alternative arrangements, as seem appropriate to the Secretary of State, for the local authority area or areas.

(2) Housing benefit

Rent officers have had a long standing involvement with housing benefit since the Housing Finance Act 1972 ('HFA 1972'). HFA 1972 permitted the rent officer to consider the rent under a contract without the consent of either landlord or tenant in order to ensure that excessive rents were not paid from public funds. This power latterly became s.68 of RA 1977 and local authorities (some more vigilantly than others) have made use of the s.68 reference as a means of protecting public funds from potential exploitation of, or collusion with, tenants in receipt of benefit. Under s.68, both landlord and tenant would be involved in the statutory procedure as if either or both of them had made the reference. The rent officer would then register a rent which would become the maximum legally recoverable rent for a period of at least two years. Appeal against the registration of this fair rent was to the RAC.

Section 68 RA 1977 has been repealed. Section 121(1) of the Act states that the Secretary of State 'may by order require rent officers to carry out such functions as may be specified ... in connection with housing benefit and rent allowance subsidy'.

Alongside this, the Social Security Act 1986 ('SSA 1986') is amended in order to allow the amount of housing benefit payable to be limited in accordance with determinations as to what rent level would be reasonable for the property, which would be made by the rent officer. This restriction on benefit may be achieved either by regulations made under s.21(6) SSA 1986 by restricting the benefit paid over to the claimant, or by limiting the housing benefit subsidy payable by central government to local authorities, where rent officer determinations show rents to be unreasonably high.

The practical effect of all this is that local authorities will be obliged to refer all housing benefit applications to the rent officers, who will not involve landlord or tenant in the deliberations. The rent officer's scrutiny will be aimed at locating rents paid within the private sector by tenants in receipt of benefit which are above the market level. In practice this can be assumed to be the average level of rent paid by those tenants who are not in receipt of benefit. In such a case, the rent officer will assess a market rent for the tenancy. This will operate to place a limit upon the rent allowance subsidy to the local authority. That authority is then free to top-up benefit from its own general rate funds. However, it must be assumed that local authorities will not do so, and as there is no requirement for the landlord to treat the rent officer determination as a ceiling, the tenant will then either have to make up the additional element of rent or seek alternative accommodation.

In order to fulfil these functions, rent officers will have the benefit of detailed regulations which will offer guidance on such questions as occupier requirements and available benefit. It is assumed that the purpose of this guidance will be to allow the rent officer to ensure that the dwelling which the claimant occupies is not more extensive than the reasonable requirements of that claimant. It is anticipated that such regulations will be introduced at a point when rent officers have accumulated sufficient evidence of market rents within their locality. There will need to be provision for the rent officer to be notified of all RAC determinations which have been made, or are due to be made, within the registration area. In order to avoid a duality of jurisdiction, a rent for an assured tenancy which has been determined by a RAC, under s.14 of the Act, will be accepted automatically as reasonable for housing benefit subsidy purposes.

Chapter 8

Tax Incentives – The Business Expansion Scheme (BES)

8.01 Introduction

The BES Scheme was introduced by the Finance Act 1983 ('FA 1983') and offers investors substantial tax incentives to invest in new and established businesses run by qualifying BES companies.

The BES Scheme, as originally devised, was seen as a method by which capital could be raised by small, high-risk businesses. In 1988 the Chancellor introduced a maximum investment limit of £500,000 per financial year in a BES company. However, there are exceptions to the £500,000 limitation including, most notably, schemes for the provision of dwelling-houses to be let upon assured tenancies under HA 1988. Up to £5,000,000 can be raised in any financial year by assured tenancy BES companies: s.290A Income and Corporation Taxes Act 1988 ('ICTA 1988') and s.50 Finance Act 1988 ('FA 1988').

Under s.50(2) FA 1988, to qualify as an assured tenancy BES company, a company must be engaged in qualifying activities which:

(a) consist of or are connected with the provision (either by the purchase of existing properties or the building of new ones) and maintenance of dwelling-houses to which this section applies which the company or subsidiary lets, or intends to let, on qualifying tenancies. 'Qualifying tenancies' are defined in s.50(3) FA 1988 to include assured tenancies other than assured shorthold tenancies and other than tenancies granted for a premium; and

(b) are, during the period beginning with the date on which the shares are issued and ending four years after that date, conducted on a commercial basis and with a view to the realisation of profits.

Section 293(2) ICTA 1988, as amended by FA 1988, states further:

'The company must, throughout the relevant period, be an unquoted company which is resident in the United Kingdom and not resident elsewhere, and be:

(a) a company which exists wholly, or substantially wholly, for the purpose of carrying on activities which do not include, to any substantial extent, activities which are non-qualifying activities; or

(b) a company whose activities consist wholly of:

   (i) the holding of shares or securities of, or the making of loans to, one or more qualifying subsidiaries of the company; or

   (ii) both the holding of such shares or securities, or the making of such loans, and the carrying on of activities which do not include to any substantial extent, activities which are not qualifying activities.'

8.02   *Individuals qualifying for relief*

There are significant tax advantages available to investors who invest in the BES Scheme. Section 291(1) ICTA 1988 states that an *individual* qualifies for the relief if he:

(a) subscribes for the eligible shares on his own behalf
(b) is resident and ordinarily resident in the United Kingdom at the time when they are issued, and
(c) is not at any time in the relevant period connected with the company

and, in relation to shares issued after 5 April 1986, an individual who is at any time performing duties which are treated by virtue of s.132(4)(a) ICTA 1988 as performed in the United Kingdom shall be treated for the purposes of this section as resident and ordinarily resident in the United Kingdom at that time.

BES is for *outside* investors, rather than for people putting money into their own business, and if a connection is shown with the company concerned relief will be disallowed.

An investor does not qualify if he or she (together with his or her close relatives, business partners and certain other 'associates') has more than 30% of the shares or the shares and loan capital or the voting power in the company (s.291 ICTA 1988). The investor must not be a paid director or an employee of the company, although he may be an unpaid director, and may receive fees for professional and similar services to the company other than as a director or employee. Neither is he allowed to be an employee nor partner of the company. Finally and specifically in relation to an assured tenancy BES company, relief will be disallowed if the investor, or his associate, occupies or is a tenant of a dwelling-house in which the company holds a superior interest.

An individual does not qualify for relief if he or she comes to a mutual agreement with someone else to invest in each other's companies. There is a general provision preventing relief being given unless the share issue is for bona fide commercial purposes and is not part of an arrangement meant to avoid tax.

The investor may only purchase new ordinary shares which have no special rights. The shares must be held for at least five years to ensure that full tax relief is retained. If the shares are disposed of earlier, some or all of the relief may be withdrawn.

It should also be noted that the BES company must not be under the control of any other company (s.292 ICTA 1988).

8.03   Tax advantages

Individuals acquiring eligible shares in qualifying companies engaged in the provision or maintenance of assured tenancies are offered the following tax incentives.

(1) Income tax

Full income tax relief is offered to individuals who take shares in qualifying companies (s.289(1) ICTA 1988). There must be a minimum investment of £500 (unless the investment is made through an approved BES fund) and a maximum of £40,000 in a tax year. Therefore, an individual paying higher rate income tax at 40% can invest a net figure of £10,000 on an outlay of £6000. If shares are disposed of within five years there will be a clawback of relief to the extent of the consideration received. However, if the disposal is made otherwise than by way of a bargain at arm's length the investor will lose all the relief previously given.

Relief is given in the year in which the shares are issued. For shares issued before 6 October in any year of assessment part of the relief can be claimed for the preceding year of assessment instead.

(2) Capital gains tax

If an investor keeps his assured tenancy company shares for five years, full capital gains tax relief will be available upon the disposal of the shares. However, if a loss arises upon disposal the investor is precluded from claiming an allowable loss against other chargeable gains.

8.04   *Limitations*

(1) It is important to realise that BES companies may only invest in dwellings with a market value of £125,000 or less in Greater London and £85,000 or less elsewhere. Market value has for these purposes a particular meaning as set out in para. 13 Schedule 4 FA 1988. In particular one has to look at the property at any time throughout the company's relevant period of four years and consider what the value would have been at the date of acquisition, assuming vacant possession and that the dwelling was then in the same condition as it is at the date of valuation (i.e. taking account of improvements) and that the locality in which the dwelling is situated was then in the same state as the date upon which the valuation takes place.

(2) It should also be noted that the BES Scheme does not apply to unfit and sub-standard dwelling-houses and dwelling-houses already let before the date when the BES company acquires an interest in them (paras 14 and 15 Schedule 4 FA 1988).

(3) The BES Scheme will not apply to any dwelling-house which was already let at the date when the company first acquired an interest.

(4) The BES Scheme does not apply to assured shorthold tenancies.

(5) The tenancies must in all respects qualify as assured tenancies. This requirement may give rise to a difficulty with the scheme in that, to remain assured, the dwelling-house must be occupied by the tenant (or at least one of joint tenants) as his only or principal home. This may prove difficult to monitor and it remains to be seen how the Inland Revenue will deal with this.

Chapter 9

Other Aspects of the Act

Part V of the Act contains a number of provisions grouped together under the heading 'Miscellaneous and General'. Of these the three which are pertinent in the context of this book relate to allowable premiums on long leases (s.115), repairing obligations in short leases (s.116) and certain amendments to the Landlord and Tenant Act 1987 (s.119 and Schedule 13). These are discussed below.

9.01 Premiums on long leases

By ss.119 and 120 RA 1977 a person who, as the condition of the grant, renewal, continuance or assignment of a Rent Act protected tenancy required the payment of any premium or the making of any loan, committed a criminal offence.

This restriction did not affect a long tenancy (i.e. a lease granted for a term certain exceeding 21 years (s.2(4) LTA 1954)) at a low rent, since a tenancy at a low rent is not protected by reason of s.5 RA 1977. Section 127 RA 1977 was designed to enable premiums and loans to be made in respect of long tenancies (s.2(4) LTA 1954 above) which were protected. Section 115 of the Act amends s.127 RA 1977 to broaden its effect. The result is that after 15 January 1989 where a tenancy is a long tenancy and protected, a loan or premium required as a condition of its grant, renewal, continuance or assignment will be allowable if the conditions summarised below are met.

The conditions are that:

(i) the landlord has no power to determine the tenancy at any time within 20 years beginning on the date when it was granted (except by way of re-entry or forfeiture for breach of any term of condition of the tenancy); and

(ii) the terms of the tenancy do not inhibit both the assignment and the underletting of the whole of the premises comprised in the tenancy (disregarding any such inhibition which applies during the final seven years of the term). By s.127(5) RA 1977 the terms of a tenancy inhibit an assignment or underletting if they:

(a) preclude it (e.g. a complete prohibition on alienation); or
(b) permit it subject to a consent but exclude s.144 LPA 1925 (no payment in the nature of fine to be exacted by a landlord whose consent is required for the grant of a licence permitting an assignment, underletting, parting with possession or disposal); or
(c) permit it subject to consent but require in connection with a request for consent the making of an offer to surrender the tenancy.

The provisions of s.115(2) are in substitution for the clauses which originally comprised s.127(2) and (3) RA 1977. Sub-sections 127(2) and (3) (*inter alia*) imposed a requirement that the rental under certain tenancies was not varied or liable to variation within 20 years of grant nor more than once in any 21 year period thereafter; this stipulation has now been swept away.

Whilst s.127(3)(C) and (D) RA 1977 have also been omitted s.127(3)(A) and (B) RA 1977 remain undisturbed so that a premium may lawfully be charged in respect of a tenancy:

 (i) which was granted before 16 July 1980
 (ii) on which a premium was lawfully required and paid on its grant
(iii) which was, at the time when it was granted, a tenancy at a low rent; and
(iv) whose terms do not inhibit both the assignment and the underletting of the whole of the premises comprised in the tenancy.

9.02   *Repairing obligations in short leases*

Section 11 LTA 1985 (in outline) implies into leases which fall within s.13 LTA 1985 (see below) a covenant on the part of the landlord:

(a) to keep in repair the structure and exterior of the dwelling (including its drains gutters and external pipes)
(b) to keep in repair and proper working order the installations in the dwelling for sanitation and for the supply of water, gas and electricity as well as those for space heating and heating water.

By s.13 LTA 1985 this obligation broadly applied to a lease of a dwelling-house granted on or after 24 October 1961 for a term of less than seven years (but see the exceptions at ss.13 and 14 LTA 1985).

The obligations in s.11 LTA 1985 are so framed as to apply to the dwelling-house and to the installations in the dwelling-house and do not direct themselves either to the structure and exterior of a block in which the dwelling-house is situated (and not forming part of the dwelling-house itself) or to installations serving but not situated in the dwelling-house: *Campden Hill Towers* v. *Gardner* [1977] 1 All ER 739.

A landlord could thus escape liability by pointing out that the defect lay not in the flat but elsewhere in the block. Section 116 attempts to overcome this and provides that where s.11 LTA 1985 applies to a lease of a dwelling-house which forms part of a building, the landlord must keep in repair the structure and exterior of 'any part of the building in which the lessor has an estate or interest'. A landlord's obligations in relation to installations have been similarly extended so that he must also keep in repair and proper working order installations serving the dwelling-house and which either form part of a building in which the landlord has an estate or interest or is owned by him or is under his control.

The circumstances in which the landlord will be liable under s.116 are, therefore, not unqualified. Furthermore, the landlord's obligation to do works only arises if the 'disrepair' ... is such as to affect the lessee's enjoyment of the dwelling-house or of any common parts ... which the lessee, as such, is entitled to use'.

The following points should also be noted:

(a) 'Common parts' means the structure and exterior of the building or part of a building and any common facilities within it: s.60(1) LTA 1987.

(b) Section 116 only applies to new leases granted on or after 15 January 1989: s.116(4).

(c) Section 116 now obliges the landlord to repair the structure and exterior of the dwelling and the structure and exterior of the common parts. The landlord is not obliged to repair common parts which are not structural or external. Such work may, however, be covered by express obligations in the tenancy agreement.

(d) The landlord has a defence to an action brought for failure to comply with his covenant to carry out works of repair if he does not have, and is unable to obtain, adequate rights to carry out the works contemplated by the section, provided that he can show that he has used all reasonable endeavours to obtain those rights: s.116(2).

9.03   *Amendments to the Landlord and Tenant Act 1987*

(1) Background to LTA 1987

The Landlord and Tenant Act 1987 (LTA 1987) passed immediately prior to the last election, implements the proposals of the Committee of Enquiry on the management of privately owned blocks of flats (Nugee Report). Although this report was primarily to look at management problems relating to privately owned blocks of flats, the legislation goes beyond these proposals, and actually enables tenants to acquire compulsorily their landlords' interest. Part I of LTA 1987, which is our primary concern, came into force on 1 February 1988, in an unamended form, notwithstanding some widespread criticism of its original drafting. The Department of the Environment is monitoring the working of the legislation, and the Secretary of State does have power to modify the LTA 1987 by making regulations under the provisions of ss.5–18 LTA 1987 (see s.20(4)). In fact certain detailed amendments have now been made to the legislation as originally drafted, but these have come in the form of s.119 and Schedule 13 of the Act. The advantage of amending the LTA 1989 in this way is to clarify the rights under the Act of the new assured tenants.

The Nugee Report found that under the general law the landlord was free to dispose of his interest in a block of flats without reference to the wishes of the tenants. Nugee found evidence of cases in which the ownership of the freehold passed through several hands in quick succession, leaving the tenants uncertain as to who their landlord was and unable to take any effective action. Whilst the Committee thought it would not be right to give the tenants a right to buy the interest of the landlord if that landlord wished to continue to own and manage the property, they were persuaded that where the landlord wishes to dispose of his interest, the tenants should have an opportunity to purchase the reversion for themselves.

(2) The effect of LTA 1987

Part I of LTA 1987 gives 'qualifying tenants' of flats a collective right of first refusal where their landlord wishes to make 'a relevant disposal' of a building or part of a building of which their flats form a part, and provided that over 50% of the flats (minimum of two) are held by 'qualifying tenants'.

A qualifying tenant is any tenant of a flat subject to certain excluded tenants. Tenants will not qualify if holding under a protected shorthold tenancy under HA 1980 or under a tenancy to which Part II of LTA 1954 applies or under a service tenancy. To this list of excluded tenants can be added all assured tenants under the 1987 Act (including assured shorthold tenants and assured agricultural occupiers) by virtue of para. 2(1) of Schedule 13 of LTA 1987.

In addition s.3 LTA 1987 as originally drafted was extremely restrictive. Essentially the section stated that a tenant would not be a qualifying tenant if he owned more than one flat or if he owned any common parts of the building. Moreover any flat which included common parts could not count towards the total of 50% necessary to trigger the landlord's duty to offer first refusal to the tenants. This created an easy avoidance device, since landlords could include very small portions of the common parts in leases of new flats. The consequences of these exclusions were that disposal notices did not need to be served, and those parts of LTA 1987 which allow for compulsory acquisition of a reversion from a landlord (who has failed to discharge his obligations relating to repair, maintenance, insurance or management of the premises, where the appointment of a manager (under Part II of LTA 1984) would seem to be an inadequate remedy) could not apply.

(3) Amendments made to LTA 1987 by the Act

By virtue of para. 2(2) Schedule 13 of the Act, excluded tenants are now tenants of the flat in question together with two or more other flats in the premises. All reference to common parts has disappeared. This ought to achieve the object of excluding tenants who are sub-letting, whilst offering the majority of tenants the necessary protections.

More importantly the position in relation to mortgages has now been clarified. Under s.4(2)(ii) LTA 1987 the disposal of 'any interest under a mortgage' is excluded from the provisions of the Act. This would have covered the transfer of a mortgage since s.4(3) provides that disposal means the disposal by the creation or the transfer of an estate or interest. However, although it was doubtless the intention to exempt from the first refusal procedure the creation of a mortgage or subsequent transfer of the benefit of the mortgage, this was not clearly achieved. The point quite simply was that until a mortgage existed, there was nothing which could be transferred 'under' it (to use the language of s.4(2)(ii) LTA 1987).

Such an interpretation would have meant that any landlord wishing to raise money on mortgage would find it necessary to offer the qualifying tenants the right to provide him with that mortgage with all the necessary procedures that Part I of LTA 1987 would entail. In order to overcome this problem para. 3(1) of Schedule 13 of the Act provides that a disposal by a mortgagee in possession (whether or not made in the name of the landlord) will be ' a relevant disposal' for the purposes of Part I of the 1987 Act.

Two avoidance devices have not been outlawed by the Act. These are the use of 'intermediate' landlords and associated companies (creating a new subsidiary transferring the reversion to it and then selling the shares in that newly created subsidiary): see further (1988) 19 EG 21; (1988) 32 EG 40. The Department of the Environment is apparently struggling to find a form of drafting which would not catch legitimate transfers within groups of companies within Part I of LTA 1987, but which could close this loophole.

The Lease/Licence Distinction

Under s.1(1) of the Act, there is a requirement of a 'tenancy' under which a dwelling is 'let' as a separate dwelling. By these two words, the lease/licence distinction which generated much case law under the Rent Acts is incorporated into the assured tenancy regime.

It is arguable that the distinction between a lease and a licence will become more important than in the past. Although assured tenancies do not attract so great a regime of regulation as Rent Act protected tenancies, a mere licence to occupy will attract none at all, not even the more limited regulation afforded to a restricted contract: they will fall through the regulatory net completely. The significance and extent of the case law on this distinction, much of it recent, justifies this separate appendix.

We may begin with the proposition that 'if ... residential accommodation is granted for a term at a rent with exclusive possession, the landlord providing neither attendance nor services, the grant is a tenancy' (see *Street* v. *Mountford* [1985] AC 809, 818 *per* Lord Templeman).

I.01 Term

Duration of the agreement is itself significant for it seems that the shorter the period, the more likely it is that the court will construe the grant as a licence rather than a lease. More than that, however, a lease must have a certain beginning and a clearly definable maximum duration. A periodic tenancy in no way offends this rule, since it can be treated as a tenancy for the stated period which, if not then determined, will run for another period. However, where the agreement is for an indefinite period, rather than a lease, there will exist a licence only.

I.02   Rent

An agreement to pay over money is a *prima facie* indication of a tenancy. It seems that the reservation of rent is not of itself vital to the existence of a tenancy (see *Ashburn Anstalt* v. *Arnold* [1988] 2 WLR 706) but what Lord Templeman appears to be saying is that where periodic payments form the consideration for the grant of exclusive possession of residential premises then the constituent elements of a tenancy are present.

I.03   Neither services nor attendance

The provision of services (see the definition in ss.19(8) and 85(1) RA 1977) is not fatal to the creation of a tenancy, but as Lord Templeman stated in *AG Securities* v. *Vaughan* [1988] 3 All ER 1058, 1065: 'if under an agreement, the owner of residential accommodation provides services of attendance and retains possession for that purpose the occupier is a lodger and the agreement creates a licence.'

This must be contrasted with the situation in which unrestricted access is not exercised: 'any express reservation to the landlord of limited rights to enter and view the state of the premises and to repair and maintain the premises only serves to emphasise the fact that the grantee is entitled to exclusive possession and is a tenant' (*per* Lord Templeman, *Street* v. *Mountford* (*supra*) at 818).

Note that on this analysis, a residential occupier is either a tenant or a lodger (c.f. *Brooker Settled Estates Ltd* v. *Ayers* (1987) 54 P & CR 165). This implies most strongly that the only available method of restricting exclusive accommodation is by the provision of services so as to create lodging. Lord Oliver would appear to support this:

'An occupier [of premises suitable for single accommodation] normally has exclusive possession ... where such possession was conceded, unless the owner retains control and unrestricted access for the purpose of providing attendance or services ... the occupier in those circumstances is either a lodger or a tenant': *AG Securities* at p.1071.

It might happen that a landlord reserves the right to move into and share a two bedroomed flat where the landlord has reason to believe that this might prove necessary, in terms of his own housing needs, in the near future. This is the type of problem which is examined in the section which follows. For now, it is necessary only to note that Lord

Oliver is beginning to look at factors beyond the tenancy agreement (*viz.* the size and type of dwelling) in order to resolve the question of the nature of the possession granted.

I.04   Exclusive possession

The problem of exclusive possession has been central to much of the confusion in the law relating to leases and licences. The basic proposition is that there cannot be a tenancy without the crucial ingredient of exclusive possession. However, the fact that the occupier enjoys exclusive possession is not of itself indicative of a tenancy. To take but one example, in *Abbeyfield (Harpenden) Society* v. *Woods* [1989] 1 WLR 374, the Court of Appeal found that, notwithstanding the occupier's exclusive possession, the arrangement was so personal in nature as to suggest a licence only. The problem with such cases is that they involve looking beyond the fact of the exclusive possession and to the intention of the parties.

In a number of cases particular difficulties have arisen because the actual intention of the parties is not reflected in the written agreement between them. This is usually because the agreement in question is drafted with the intention of evading the Rent Acts. It is open to the parties to arrange their affairs so as not to create a Rent Act protected tenancy, but where this is done by an entirely artificial device which does not reflect the reality of the bargain between the parties, it is open for the courts to set such documents aside.

(1)   Sham agreements

A non-exclusive occupation agreement is an agreement which gives the occupier the right to use the premises but only in conjunction with such other persons who may share a similar right. The aim is to prevent any one occupier gaining exclusive possession of any part of the premises, thereby denying the possibility of a tenancy. In *Somma* v. *Hazlehurst* [1978] 1 WLR 1014 this type of agreement was said to give rise to a licence where an unmarried couple entered into separate agreements to share a double bed-sitting room. In particular, it was said that the right which the owner reserved to introduce another licensee on the departure of either of the occupants was inconsistent with a grant of exclusive possession.

The case was disapproved in *Street* v. *Mountford* (*supra*) which urged the courts to 'be astute to detect and frustrate sham devices and artificial transactions whose only object is to disguise the grant of a tenancy and to evade the Rent Acts'. This begs the question of how one recognises a sham agreement or artificial transaction, but *Street* began from the premise that where the consequence of an agreement is exclusive occupation for a term, at a rent, then, irrespective of the declared intention of the parties, that agreement is presumed to constitute a lease. Thereafter it was open to the court to examine the nature of the arrangement between the parties so as to determine whether the terms of any agreement reflect the reality.

In *Hadjiloucas* v. *Crean* [1987] 3 All ER 1008, the Court of Appeal pointed to the ability of the courts to determine whether a document which, on its face, suggests a licence actually falls, in the light of surrounding circumstances, into the category of lease. However, more specific guidance as to what such circumstances should be were lacking, and in marginal cases, particularly those relating to accommodation which was shared, the *Street* approach left a number of matters unresolved.

(2) Shared accommodation

The appeals in the cases of *AG Securities* v. *Vaughan* and *Antoniades* v. *Villiers* were heard together in the House of Lords, although they involved quite different facts and had been held in the Court of Appeal to concern a joint tenancy and a licence (respectively) prior to the House of Lords reversing both decisions. Both cases involved occupiers of shared premises each of whom were given separate agreements, which stated that additional persons could be allowed to share the premises.

In *Villiers* there were two sharers – an unmarried couple – who made a joint approach to the landlord and were given agreements which had the same commencement dates, term and rent. In *Vaughan*, the sharers were strangers each of whom approached the landlord individually to be given separate agreements which showed no commonality of date, term or rent. In finding that the *Villiers* arrangements constituted a joint tenancy, whereas those in *Vaughan* resulted in a series of licences, it is clear that the House of Lords looked beyond the face of the separate agreements.

In doing so, the House of Lords looked at the background to the agreement including the relationship of the sharers and the nature of the property. The operation of the agreement was also examined: 'the intended and actual mode of occupation'. Their Lordships stressed that while knowledge of the operation of the agreement could not be used to interpret that agreement, it could be used to assess its genuineness.

This might work to expose the agreement as a 'pretence' the intended purpose of which was to outflank protective legislation. On the other hand it might operate to prove the reality of the agreement as drafted. In *Stribling* v. *Wickham* [1989] EGCS 41, a four roomed flat consisting initially of two bedrooms, one sitting room and one dining room was let to three friends under three agreements purporting to be licences. Two of the original parties left to be replaced by two other occupants, although for a time the flat was occupied by two persons only. When the appellant landlord sought to recover possession, the Court of Appeal had little hesitation in following *Vaughan* and holding that the agreements represented the realities of a transaction which was a genuine and sensible arrangement of benefit to all parties.

However, although the House of Lords is willing to examine the operation of the agreement, Lord Templeman denies this possibility in another sense. In his view, although there was apparently the power in the agreement in *Antoniades* to nominate other occupiers,

'until that power is exercised [the occupiers] are jointly in exclusive occupation of the whole flat making periodic payments and are therefore tenants. The Rent Act prevents the exercise of a power which would destroy the tenancy of [the occupiers] and would deprive them of the exclusive occupation which they are now enjoying.'

If this analysis is correct, it would never be possible for the landlord to reserve a right to later take up occupation of the premises. It is submitted that this cannot be so, and that it must be possible to have a genuine agreement that, although the occupiers will enjoy initially exclusive occupation, later the landlord will take up residence.

On the other hand, Lord Templeman is clearly correct in asserting that the reservation of a right which, if exercised, would determine what is clearly a tenancy will be inconsistent with protective legislation and cannot be enforced:

'Were it otherwise, every tenancy agreement would be labelled a licence and would contract out of the Rent Acts by reserving power to the landlord to share possession with the tenant at any time after commencement of the term.'

I.05   *Conclusion*

The grant of exclusive occupation, for a term, at a rent gives rise to a tenancy in the absence of other factors which indicate lodging. In determining whether agreements constitute a lease or a licence, the courts will apply the above test, but, if necessary, by going beyond the face of the agreement and examining the rights and duties which arise in reality. This may necessitate the courts examining the actual operation of the agreement taking into account factors which relate to the nature of the parties to the agreement and dwelling subject to it.

This process is an attempt to expose agreements which represent a 'pretence' in order that protective legislation is defeated. The courts will be vigilant and will refuse to enforce any provision in an agreement which will have the effect of denying statutory protection to a tenant. In attaching the label 'tenant' the courts will act so as not to permit parties to contract out of the protective legislation whilst allowing that there are occasions when parties may have genuinely intended no more than a licence.

Appendix II

Housing Act 1988:
Relevant Sections

Meaning of assured tenancy etc.

Assured tenancies

1.—(1) A tenancy under which a dwelling-house is let as a separate dwelling is for the purposes of this Act an assured tenancy if and so long as—

(a) the tenant or, as the case may be, each of the joint tenants is an individual; and

(b) the tenant or, as the case may be, at least one of the joint tenants occupies the dwelling-house as his only or principal home; and

(c) the tenancy is not one which, by virtue of subsection (2) or subsection (6) below, cannot be an assured tenancy.

(2) Subject to subsection (3) below, if and so long as a tenancy falls within any paragraph in Part I of Schedule 1 to this Act, it cannot be an assured tenancy; and in that Schedule—

(a) "tenancy" means a tenancy under which a dwelling-house is let as a separate dwelling;

(b) Part II has effect for determining the rateable value of a dwelling-house for the purposes of Part I; and

(c) Part III has effect for supplementing paragraph 10 in Part I.

(3) Except as provided in Chapter V below, at the commencement of this Act, a tenancy—

(a) under which a dwelling-house was then let as a separate dwelling; and

(b) which immediately before that commencement was an assured tenancy for the purposes of sections 56 to 58 of the Housing Act 1980 (tenancies granted by approved bodies),

shall become an assured tenancy for the purposes of this Act.

(4) In relation to an assured tenancy falling within subsection (3) above—

(a) Part I of Schedule 1 to this Act shall have effect, subject to subsection (5) below, as if it consisted only of paragraphs 11 and 12; and

(b) sections 56 to 58 of the Housing Act 1980 (and Schedule 5 to that Act) shall not apply after the commencement of this Act.

(5) In any case where—

(a) immediately before the commencement of this Act the landlord under a tenancy is a fully mutual housing association, and

(b) at the commencement of this Act the tenancy becomes an assured tenancy by virtue of subsection (3) above,

then, so long as that association remains the landlord under that tenancy (and under any statutory periodic tenancy which arises on the coming to an end of that tenancy), paragraph 12 of Schedule 1 to this Act shall have effect in relation to that tenancy with the omission of sub-paragraph (1)(h).

(6) If, in pursuance of its duty under—

(a) section 63 of the Housing Act 1985 (duty to house pending inquiries in case of apparent priority need),

(b) section 65(3) of that Act (duty to house temporarily person found to have priority need but to have become homeless intentionally), or

(c) section 68(1) of that Act (duty to house pending determination whether conditions for referral of application are satisfied),

a local housing authority have made arrangements with another person to provide accommodation, a tenancy granted by that other person in pursuance of the arrangements to a person specified by the authority cannot be an assured tenancy before the expiry of the period of twelve months beginning with the date specified in subsection (7) below unless, before the expiry of that period, the tenant is notified by the landlord (or, in the case of joint landlords, at least one of them) that the tenancy is to be regarded as an assured tenancy.

(7) The date referred to in subsection (6) above is the date on which the tenant received the notification required by section 64(1) of the Housing Act 1985 (notification of decision on question of homelessness or threatened homelessness) or, if he received a notification under section 68(3) of that Act (notification of which authority has duty to house), the date on which he received that notification.

Letting of a dwelling-house together with other land
2.—(1) If, under a tenancy, a dwelling-house is let together with other land, then, for the purposes of this Part of this Act,—

(a) if and so long as the main purpose of the letting is the provision of a home for the tenant or, where there are joint tenants, at least one of them, the other land shall be treated as part of the dwelling-house; and

(b) if and so long as the main purpose of the letting is not as mentioned in paragraph (a) above, the tenancy shall be treated as not being one under which a dwelling-house is let as a separate dwelling.

(2) Nothing in subsection (1) above affects any question whether a tenancy is precluded from being an assured tenancy by virtue of any provision of Schedule 1 to this Act.

Tenant sharing accommodation with persons other than landlord
3.—(1) Where a tenant has the exclusive occupation of any accommodation (in this section referred to as "the separate accommodation") and—

(a) the terms as between the tenant and his landlord on which he holds the separate accommodation include the use of other accommodation (in this section referred to as "the shared accommodation") in common with another person or other persons, not being or including the landlord, and

(b) by reason only of the circumstances mentioned in paragraph (a) above, the separate accommodation would not, apart from this section, be a dwelling-house let on an assured tenancy,

the separate accommodation shall be deemed to be a dwelling-house let on an assured tenancy and the following provisions of this section shall have effect.

(2) For the avoidance of doubt it is hereby declared that where, for the purpose of determining the rateable value of the separate accommodation, it is necessary to make an apportionment under Part II of Schedule 1 to this Act, regard is to be had to the circumstances mentioned in subsection (1)(a) above.

(3) While the tenant is in possession of the separate accommodation, any term of the tenancy terminating or modifying, or providing for the termination or modification of, his right to the use of any of the shared accommodation which is living accommodation shall be of no effect.

(4) Where the terms of the tenancy are such that, at any time during the tenancy, the persons in common with whom the tenant is entitled to the use of the shared accommodation could be varied or their number could be increased, nothing in subsection (3) above shall prevent those terms from having effect so far as they relate to any such variation or increase.

(5) In this section "living accommodation" means accommodation of such a nature that the fact that it constitutes or is included in the shared accommodation is sufficient, apart from this section, to prevent the tenancy from constituting an assured tenancy of a dwelling-house.

Certain sublettings not to exclude any part of sublessor's premises from assured tenancy
4.—(1) Where the tenant of a dwelling-house has sub-let a part but not the whole of the dwelling-house, then, as against his landlord or any superior landlord, no part of the dwelling-house shall be treated as excluded from being a dwelling-house let on an assured tenancy by reason only that the terms on which any person claiming under the tenant holds any part of the dwelling-house include the use of accommodation in common with other persons.

(2) Nothing in this section affects the rights against, and liabilities to, each other of the tenant and any person claiming under him, or of any two such persons.

Security of tenure

5.—(1) An assured tenancy cannot be brought to an end by the landlord except by obtaining an order of the court in accordance with the following provisions of this Chapter or Chapter II below or, in the case of a fixed term tenancy which contains power for the landlord to determine the tenancy in certain circumstances, by the exercise of that power and, accordingly, the service by the landlord of a notice to quit shall be of no effect in relation to a periodic assured tenancy.

(2) If an assured tenancy which is a fixed term tenancy comes to an end otherwise than by virtue of—

(a) an order of the court, or

(b) a surrender or other action on the part of the tenant,

then, subject to section 7 and Chapter II below, the tenant shall be entitled to remain in possession of the dwelling-house let under that tenancy and, subject to subsection (4) below, his right to possession shall depend upon a periodic tenancy arising by virtue of this section.

(3) The periodic tenancy referred to in subsection (2) above is one—

(a) taking effect in possession immediately on the coming to an end of the fixed term tenancy;

(b) deemed to have been granted by the person who was the landlord under the fixed term tenancy immediately before it came to an end to the person who was then the tenant under that tenancy;

(c) under which the premises which are let are the same dwelling-house as was let under the fixed term tenancy;

(d) under which the periods of the tenancy are the same as those for which rent was last payable under the fixed term tenancy; and

(e) under which, subject to the following provisions of this Part of this Act, the other terms are the same as those of the fixed term tenancy immediately before it came to an end, except that any term which makes provision for determination by the landlord or the tenant shall not have effect while the tenancy remains an assured tenancy.

(4) The periodic tenancy referred to in subsection (2) above shall not arise if, on the coming to an end of the fixed term tenancy, the tenant is entitled, by virtue of the grant of another tenancy, to possession of the same or substantially the same dwelling-house as was let to him under the fixed term tenancy.

(5) If, on or before the date on which a tenancy is entered into or is deemed to have been granted as mentioned in subsection (3)(b) above, the person who is to be the tenant under that tenancy—

(a) enters into an obligation to do any act which (apart from this subsection) will cause the tenancy to come to an end at a time when it is an assured tenancy, or

(b) executes, signs or gives any surrender, notice to quit or other document which (apart from this subsection) has the effect of bringing the tenancy to an end at a time when it is an assured tenancy.

the obligation referred to in paragraph (a) above shall not be enforceable or, as the case may be, the surrender, notice to quit or other document referred to in paragraph (b) above shall be of no effect.

(6) If, by virtue of any provision of this Part of this Act, Part I of Schedule 1 to this Act has effect in relation to a fixed term tenancy as if it consisted only of paragraphs 11 and 12, that Part shall have the like effect in relation to any periodic tenancy which arises by virtue of this section on the coming to an end of the fixed term tenancy.

(7) Any reference in this Part of this Act to a statutory periodic tenancy is a reference to a periodic tenancy arising by virtue of this section.

Fixing of terms of statutory periodic tenancy

6.—(1) In this section, in relation to a statutory periodic tenancy,—

(a) "the former tenancy" means the fixed term tenancy on the coming to an end of which the statutory periodic tenancy arises; and

(b) "the implied terms" means the terms of the tenancy which have effect by virtue of section 5(3)(e) above, other than terms as to the amount of the rent;

but nothing in the following provisions of this section applies to a statutory periodic tenancy at a time when, by virtue of paragraph 11 or paragraph 12 in Part 1 of Schedule 1 to this Act, it cannot be an assured tenancy.

(2) Not later than the first anniversary of the day on which the former tenancy came to an end, the landlord may serve on the tenant, or the tenant may serve on the landlord, a notice in the prescribed form proposing terms of the statutory periodic tenancy different from the implied terms and, if the landlord or the tenant considers it appropriate, proposing an adjustment of the amount of the rent to take account of the proposed terms.

(3) Where a notice has been served under subsection (2) above,—

(a) within the period of three months beginning on the date on which the notice was served on him, the landlord or the tenant, as the case may be, may, by an application in the prescribed form, refer the notice to a rent assessment committee under subsection (4) below; and

(b) if the notice is not so referred, then, with effect from such date, not falling within the period referred to in paragraph (a) above, as may be specified in the notice, the terms proposed in the notice shall become terms of the tenancy in substitution for any of the implied terms dealing with the same subject matter and the amount of the rent shall be varied in accordance with any adjustment so proposed.

(4) Where a notice under subsection (2) above is referred to a rent assessment committee, the committee shall consider the terms proposed in the notice and shall determine whether those terms, or some other terms (dealing with the same subject matter as the proposed terms), are such as, in the committee's opinion, might reasonably be expected to be found in an assured periodic tenancy of the dwelling-house concerned, being a tenancy—

(a) which begins on the coming to an end of the former tenancy; and

(b) which is granted by a willing landlord on terms which, except in so far as they relate to the subject matter of the proposed terms, are those of the statutory periodic tenancy at the time of the committee's consideration.

(5) Whether or not a notice under subsection (2) above proposes an adjustment of the amount of the rent under the statutory periodic tenancy, where a rent assessment committee determine any terms under subsection (4) above, they shall, if they consider it appropriate, specify such an adjustment to take account of the terms so determined.

(6) In making a determination under subsection (4) above, or specifying an adjustment of an amount of rent under subsection (5) above, there shall be disregarded any effect on the terms or the amount of the rent attributable to the granting of a tenancy to a sitting tenant.

(7) Where a notice under subsection (2) above is referred to a rent assessment committee, then, unless the landlord and the tenant otherwise agree, with effect from such date as the committee may direct—

(a) the terms determined by the committee shall become terms of the statutory periodic tenancy in substitution for any of the implied terms dealing with the same subject matter; and

(b) the amount of the rent under the statutory periodic tenancy shall be altered to accord with any adjustment specified by the committee;

but for the purposes of paragraph (b) above the committee shall not direct a date earlier than the date specified, in accordance with subsection (3)(b) above, in the notice referred to them.

(8) Nothing in this section requires a rent assessment committee to continue with a determination under subsection (4) above if the landlord and tenant give notice in writing that they no longer require such a determination or if the tenancy has come to an end.

Order for possession

7.—(1) The court shall not make an order for possession of a dwelling-house let on an assured tenancy except on one or more of the grounds set out in Schedule 2 to this Act; but nothing in this Part of this Act relates to proceedings for possession of such a dwelling-house which are brought by a mortgagee, within the meaning of the Law of Property Act 1925, who has lent money on the security of the assured tenancy.

(2) The following provisions of this section have effect, subject to section 8 below, in relation to proceedings for the recovery of possession of a dwelling-house let on an assured tenancy.

(3) If the court is satisfied that any of the grounds in Part I of Schedule 2 to this Act is established then, subject to subsection (6) below, the court shall make an order for possession.

(4) If the court is satisfied that any of the grounds in Part II of Schedule 2 to this Act is established, then, subject to subsection (6) below, the court may make an order for possession if it considers it reasonable to do so.

(5) Part III of Schedule 2 to this Act shall have effect for supplementing Ground 9 in that Schedule and Part IV of that Schedule shall have effect in relation to notices given as mentioned in Grounds 1 to 5 of that Schedule.

(6) The court shall not make an order for possession of a dwelling-house to take effect at a time when it is let on an assured fixed term tenancy unless—

  (a) the ground for possession is Ground 2 or Ground 8 in Part I of Schedule 2 to this Act or any of the grounds in Part II of that Schedule, other than Ground 9 or Ground 16; and

  (b) the terms of the tenancy make provision for it to be brought to an end on the ground in question (whether that provision takes the form of a provision for re-entry, for forfeiture, for determination by notice or otherwise).

(7) Subject to the preceding provisions of this section, the court may make an order for possession of a dwelling-house on grounds relating to a fixed term tenancy which has come to an end; and where an order is made in such circumstances, any statutory periodic tenancy which has arisen on the ending of the fixed term tenancy shall end (without any notice and regardless of the period) on the day on which the order takes effect.

Notice of proceedings for possession

8.—(1) The court shall not entertain proceedings for possession of a dwelling-house let on an assured tenancy unless—

  (a) the landlord or, in the case of joint landlords, at least one of them has served on the tenant a notice in accordance with this section and the proceedings are begun within the time limits stated in the notice in accordance with subsections (3) and (4) below; or

(b) the court considers it just and equitable to dispense with the requirement of such a notice.

(2) The court shall not make an order for possession on any of the grounds in Schedule 2 to this Act unless that ground and particulars of it are specified in the notice under this section; but the grounds specified in such a notice may be altered or added to with the leave of the court.

(3) A notice under this section is one in the prescribed form informing the tenant that—

(a) the landlord intends to begin proceedings for possession of the dwelling-house on one or more of the grounds specified in the notice; and

(b) those proceedings will not begin earlier than a date specified in the notice which, without prejudice to any additional limitation under subsection (4) below, shall not be earlier than the expiry of the period of two weeks from the date of service of the notice; and

(c) those proceedings will not begin later than twelve months from the date of service of the notice.

(4) If a notice under this section specifies, in accordance with subsection (3)(a) above, any of Grounds 1, 2, 5 to 7, 9 and 16 in Schedule 2 to this Act (whether with or without other grounds), the date specified in the notice as mentioned in subsection (3)(b) above shall not be earlier than—

(a) two months from the date of service of the notice; and

(b) if the tenancy is a periodic tenancy, the earliest date on which, apart from section 5(1) above, the tenancy could be brought to an end by a notice to quit given by the landlord on the same date as the date of service of the notice under this section.

(5) The court may not exercise the power conferred by subsection (1)(b) above if the landlord seeks to recover possession on Ground 8 in Schedule 2 to this Act.

(6) Where a notice under this section—

(a) is served at a time when the dwelling-house is let on a fixed term tenancy, or

(b) is served after a fixed term tenancy has come to an end but relates (in whole or in part) to events occurring during that tenancy,

the notice shall have effect notwithstanding that the tenant becomes or has become tenant under a statutory periodic tenancy arising on the coming to an end of the fixed term tenancy.

Extended discretion of court in possession claims

9.—(1) Subject to subsection (6) below, the court may adjourn for such period or periods as it thinks fit proceedings for possession of a dwelling-house let on an assured tenancy.

(2) On the making of an order for possession of a dwelling-house let on an assured tenancy or at any time before the execution of such an order, the court, subject to subsection (6) below, may—

(a) stay or suspend execution of the order, or

(b) postpone the date of possession,

for such period or periods as the court thinks just.

(3) On any such adjournment as is referred to in subsection (1) above or on any such stay, suspension or postponement as is referred to in subsection (2) above, the court, unless it considers that to do so would cause exceptional hardship to the tenant or would otherwise be unreasonable, shall impose conditions with regard to payment by the tenant of arrears of rent (if any) and rent or payments in respect of occupation after the termination of the tenancy (mesne profits) and may impose such other conditions as it thinks fit.

(4) If any such conditions as are referred to in subsection (3) above are complied with, the court may, if it thinks fit, discharge or rescind any such order as is referred to in subsection (2) above.

(5) In any case where—

    (a) at a time when proceedings are brought for possession of a dwelling-house let on an assured tenancy, the tenant's spouse or former spouse, having rights of occupation under the Matrimonial Homes Act 1983, is in occupation of the dwelling-house, and

    (b) the assured tenancy is terminated as a result of those proceedings,

the spouse or former spouse, so long as he or she remains in occupation, shall have the same rights in relation to, or in connection with, any such adjournment as is referred to in subsection (1) above or any such stay, suspension or postponement as is referred to in subsection (2) above, as he or she would have if those rights of occupation were not affected by the termination of the tenancy.

(6) This section does not apply if the court is satisfied that the landlord is entitled to possession of the dwelling-house—

    (a) on any of the grounds in Part I of Schedule 2 to this Act; or

    (b) by virtue of subsection (1) or subsection (4) of section 21 below.

Special provisions applicable to shared accommodation

10.—(1) This section applies in a case falling within subsection (1) of section 3 above and expressions used in this section have the same meaning as in that section.

(2) Without prejudice to the enforcement of any order made under subsection (3) below, while the tenant is in possession of the separate accommodation, no order shall be made for possession of any of the shared accommodation, whether on the application of the immediate landlord of the tenant or on the application of any person under whom that landlord derives title, unless a like order has been made, or is made at the same time, in respect of the separate accommodation; and the provisions of section 6 above shall have effect accordingly.

(3) On the application of the landlord, the court may make such order as it thinks just either—

    (a) terminating the right of the tenant to use the whole or any part of the shared accommodation other than living accommodation; or

    (b) modifying his right to use the whole or any part of the shared accommodation, whether by varying the persons or increasing the number of persons entitled to the use of that accommodation or otherwise.

(4) No order shall be made under subsection (3) above so as to effect any termination or modification of the rights of the tenant which, apart from section 3(3) above, could not be effected by or under the terms of the tenancy.

Payment of removal expenses in certain cases

11.—(1) Where a court makes an order for possession of a dwelling-house let on an assured tenancy on Ground 6 or Ground 9 in Schedule 2 to this Act (but not on any other ground), the landlord shall pay to the tenant a sum equal to the reasonable expenses likely to be incurred by the tenant in removing from the dwelling-house.

(2) Any question as to the amount of the sum referred to in subsection (1) above shall be determined by agreement between the landlord and the tenant or, in default of agreement, by the court.

(3) Any sum payable to a tenant by virtue of this section shall be recoverable as a civil debt due from the landlord.

Compensation for misrepresentation or concealment

12. Where a landlord obtains an order for possession of a dwelling-house let on an assured tenancy on one or more of the grounds in Schedule 2 to this Act and it is subsequently made to appear to the court that the order was obtained by misrepresentation or concealment of material facts, the court may order the landlord to pay to the former tenant such sum as appears sufficient as compensation for damage or loss sustained by that tenant as a result of the order.

Rent and other terms

Increases of rent under assured periodic tenancies

13.—(1) This section applies to—

(a) a statutory periodic tenancy other than one which, by virtue of paragraph 11 or paragraph 12 in Part I of Schedule 1 to this Act, cannot for the time being be an assured tenancy; and

(b) any other periodic tenancy which is an assured tenancy, other than one in relation to which there is a provision, for the time being binding on the tenant, under which the rent for a particular period of the tenancy will or may be greater than the rent for an earlier period.

(2) For the purpose of securing an increase in the rent under a tenancy to which this section applies, the landlord may serve on the tenant a notice in the prescribed form proposing a new rent to take effect at the beginning of a new period of the tenancy specified in the notice, being a period beginning not earlier than—

(a) the minimum period after the date of the service of the notice; and

(b) except in the case of a statutory periodic tenancy, the first anniversary of the date on which the first period of the tenancy began; and

(c) if the rent under the tenancy has previously been increased by virtue of a notice under this subsection or a determination under section 14 below, the first anniversary of the date on which the increased rent took effect.

(3) The minimum period referred to in subsection (2) above is—

(a) in the case of a yearly tenancy, six months;

(b) in the case of a tenancy where the period is less than a month, one month; and

(c) in any other case, a period equal to the period of the tenancy.

(4) Where a notice is served under subsection 2 above, a new rent specified in the notice shall take effect as mentioned in the notice unless, before the beginning of the new period specified in the notice,—

(a) the tenant by an application in the prescribed form refers the notice to a rent assessment committee; or

(b) the landlord and the tenant agree on a variation of the rent which is different from that proposed in the notice or agree that the rent should not be varied.

(5) Nothing in this section (or in section 14 below) affects the right of the landlord and the tenant under an assured tenancy to vary by agreement any term of the tenancy (including a term relating to rent).

Determination of rent by rent assessment committee

14.—(1) Where, under subsection (4)(a) of section 13 above, a tenant refers to a rent assessment committee a notice under subsection (2) of that section, the committee shall determine the rent at which, subject to subsections (2) and (4) below, the committee consider that the dwelling-house concerned might reasonably be expected to be let in the open market by a willing landlord under an assured tenancy—

(a) which is a periodic tenancy having the same periods as those of the tenancy to which the notice relates;

(b) which begins at the beginning of the new period specified in the notice;

(c) the terms of which (other than relating to the amount of the rent) are the same as those of the tenancy to which the notice relates; and

(d) in respect of which the same notices, if any, have been given under any of Grounds 1 to 5 of Schedule 2 to this Act, as have been given (or have effect as if given) in relation to the tenancy to which the notice relates.

(2) In making a determination under this section, there shall be disregarded—

(a) any effect on the rent attributable to the granting of a tenancy to a sitting tenant;

(b) any increase in the value of the dwelling-house attributable to a relevant improvement carried out by a person who at the time it was carried out was the tenant, if the improvement—

(i) was carried out otherwise than in pursuance of an obligation to his immediate landlord, or

(ii) was carried out pursuant to an obligation to his immediate landlord being an obligation which did not relate to the specific improvement concerned but arose by reference to consent given to the carrying out of that improvement; and

(c) any reduction in the value of the dwelling-house attributable to a failure by the tenant to comply with any terms of the tenancy.

(3) For the purposes of subsection (2)(b) above, in relation to a notice which is referred by a tenant as mentioned in subsection (1) above, an improvement is a relevant improvement if either it was carried out during the tenancy to which the notice relates or the following conditions are satisfied, namely—

(a) that it was carried out not more than twenty-one years before the date of service of the notice; and

(b) that, at all times during the period beginning when the improvement was carried out and ending on the date of service of the notice, the dwelling-house has been let under an assured tenancy; and

(c) that, on the coming to an end of an assured tenancy at any time during that period, the tenant (or, in the case of joint tenants, at least one of them) did not quit.

(4) In this section "rent" does not include any service charge, within the meaning of section 18 of the Landlord and Tenant Act 1985, but, subject to that, includes any sums payable by the tenant to the landlord on account of the use of furniture or for any of the matters referred to in subsection (1)(a) of that section, whether or not those sums are separate from the sums payable for the occupation of the dwelling-house concerned or are payable under separate agreements.

(5) Where any rates in respect of the dwelling-house concerned are borne by the landlord or a superior landlord, the rent assessment committee shall make their determination under this section as if the rates were not so borne.

(6) In any case where—

(a) a rent assessment committee have before them at the same time the reference of a notice under section 6(2) above relating to a tenancy (in this subsection referred to as "the section 6 reference") and the reference of a notice under section 13(2) above relating to the same tenancy (in this subsection referred to as "the section 13 reference"), and

(b) the date specified in the notice under section 6(2) above is not later than the first day of the new period specified in the notice under section 13(2) above, and

(c) the committee propose to hear the two references together,

the committee shall make a determination in relation to the section 6 reference before making their determination in relation to the section 13 reference and, accordingly, in such a case the reference in subsection (1)(c) above to the terms of the tenancy to which the notice relates shall be construed as a reference to those terms as varied by virtue of the determination made in relation to the section 6 reference.

(7) Where a notice under section 13(2) above has been referred to a rent assessment committee, then, unless the landlord and the tenant otherwise agree, the rent determined by the committee (subject, in a case where subsection (5) above applies, to the addition of the appropriate amount in respect of rates) shall be the rent under the tenancy with effect from the beginning of the new period specified in the notice or, if it appears to the rent assessment committee that that would cause undue hardship to the tenant, with effect from such later date (not being later than the date the rent is determined) as the committee may direct.

(8) Nothing in this section requires a rent assessment committee to continue with their determination of a rent for a dwelling-house if the landlord and tenant give notice in writing that they no longer require such a determination or if the tenancy has come to an end.

Limited prohibition on assignment etc. without consent

15.—(1) Subject to subsection (3) below, it shall be an implied term of every assured tenancy which is a periodic tenancy that, except with the consent of the landlord, the tenant shall not—

(a) assign the tenancy (in whole or in part); or

(b) sub-let or part with possession of the whole or any part of the dwelling-house let on the tenancy.

(2) Section 19 of the Landlord and Tenant Act 1927 (consents to assign not to be

unreasonably withheld etc.) shall not apply to a term which is implied into an assured tenancy by subsection (1) above.

(3) In the case of a periodic tenancy which is not a statutory periodic tenancy subsection (1) above does not apply if—

(a) there is a provision (whether contained in the tenancy or not) under which the tenant is prohibited (whether absolutely or conditionally) from assigning or sub-letting or parting with possession or is permitted (whether absolutely or conditionally) to assign, sub-let or part with possession; or

(b) a premium is required to be paid on the grant or renewal of the tenancy.

(4) In subsection (3)(b) above "premium" includes—

(a) any fine or other like sum;

(b) any other pecuniary consideration in addition to rent; and

(c) any sum paid by way of deposit, other than one which does not exceed one-sixth of the annual rent payable under the tenancy immediately after the grant or renewal in question.

Access for repairs

16. It shall be an implied term of every assured tenancy that the tenant shall afford to the landlord access to the dwelling-house let on the tenancy and all reasonable facilities for executing therein any repairs which the landlord is entitled to execute.

Miscellaneous

Succession to assured periodic tenancy by spouse

17.—(1) In any case where—

(a) the sole tenant under an assured periodic tenancy dies, and

(b) immediately before the death, the tenant's spouse was occupying the dwelling-house as his or her only or principal home, and

(c) the tenant was not himself a successor, as defined in subsection (2) or subsection (3) below,

then, on the death, the tenancy vests by virtue of this section in the spouse (and, accordingly, does not devolve under the tenant's will or intestacy).

(2) For the purposes of this section, a tenant is a successor in relation to a tenancy if—

(a) the tenancy became vested in him either by virtue of this section or under the will or intestacy of a previous tenant; or

(b) at some time before the tenant's death the tenancy was a joint tenancy held by himself and one or more other persons and, prior to his death, he became the sole tenant by survivorship; or

(c) he became entitled to the tenancy as mentioned in section 39(5) below.

(3) For the purposes of this section, a tenant is also a successor in relation to a tenancy (in this subsection referred to as "the new tenancy") which was granted to him (alone or jointly with others) if—

(a) at some time before the grant of the new tenancy, he was, by virtue of subsection (2) above, a successor in relation to an earlier tenancy of the same or substantially the same dwelling-house as is let under the new tenancy; and

(b) at all times since he became such a successor he has been a tenant (alone or jointly with others) of the dwelling-house which is let under the new tenancy or of a dwelling-house which is substantially the same as that dwelling-house.

(4) For the purposes of this section, a person who was living with the tenant as his or her wife or husband shall be treated as the tenant's spouse.

(5) If, on the death of the tenant, there is, by virtue of subsection (4) above, more than one person who fulfils the condition in subsection (1)(b) above, such one of them as may be decided by agreement or, in default of agreement, by the county court shall be treated as the tenant's spouse for the purposes of this section.

Provisions as to reversions on assured tenancies
18.—(1) If at any time—

(a) a dwelling-house is for the time being lawfully let on an assured tenancy, and

(b) the landlord under the assured tenancy is himself a tenant under a superior tenancy; and

(c) the superior tenancy comes to an end,

then, subject to subsection (2) below, the assured tenancy shall continue in existence as a tenancy held of the person whose interest would, apart from the continuance of the assured tenancy, entitle him to actual possession of the dwelling-house at that time.

(2) Subsection (1) above does not apply to an assured tenancy if the interest which, by virtue of that subsection, would become that of the landlord, is such that, by virtue of Schedule 1 to this Act, the tenancy could not be an assured tenancy.

(3) Where, by virtue of any provision of this Part of this Act, an assured tenancy which is a periodic tenancy (including a statutory periodic tenancy) continues beyond the beginning of a reversionary tenancy which was granted (whether before, on or after the commencement of this Act) so as to begin on or after—

(a) the date on which the previous contractual assured tenancy came to an end, or

(b) a date on which, apart from any provision of this Part, the periodic tenancy could have been brought to an end by the landlord by notice to quit,

the reversionary tenancy shall have effect as if it had been granted subject to the periodic tenancy.

(4) The reference in subsection (3) above to the previous contractual assured tenancy applies only where the periodic tenancy referred to in that subsection is a statutory periodic tenancy and is a reference to the fixed-term tenancy which immediately preceded the statutory periodic tenancy.

Restriction on levy of distress for rent
19.—(1) Subject to subsection (2) below, no distress for the rent of any dwelling-house let on an assured tenancy shall be levied except with the leave of the county court; and, with respect to any application for such leave, the court shall have the same powers with respect to adjournment, stay, suspension, postponement and otherwise as are conferred by section 9 above in relation to proceedings for possession of such a dwelling-house.

(2) Nothing in subsection (1) above applies to distress levied under section 102 of the County Courts Act 1984.

20.—(1) Subject to subsection (3) below, an assured shorthold tenancy is an assured tenancy—

(a) which is a fixed term tenancy granted for a term certain of not less than six months; and

(b) in respect of which there is no power for the landlord to determine the tenancy at any time earlier than six months from the beginning of the tenancy; and

(c) in respect of which a notice is served as mentioned in subsection (2) below.

(2) The notice referred to in subsection (1)(c) above is one which—

(a) is in such form as may be prescribed;

(b) is served before the assured tenancy is entered into;

(c) is served by the person who is to be the landlord under the assured tenancy on the person who is to be the tenant under that tenancy; and

(d) states that the assured tenancy to which it relates is to be a shorthold tenancy.

(3) Notwithstanding anything in subsection (1) above, where—

(a) immediately before a tenancy (in this subsection referred to as "the new tenancy") is granted, the person to whom it is granted or, as the case may be, at least one of the persons to whom it is granted was a tenant under an assured tenancy which was not a shorthold tenancy, and

(b) the new tenancy is granted by the person who, immediately before the beginning of the tenancy, was the landlord under the assured tenancy referred to in paragraph (a) above,

the new tenancy cannot be an assured shorthold tenancy.

(4) Subject to subsection (5) below, if, on the coming to an end of an assured shorthold tenancy (including a tenancy which was an assured shorthold but ceased to be assured before it came to an end), a new tenancy of the same or substantially the same premises comes into being under which the landlord and the tenant are the same as at the coming to an end of the earlier tenancy, then, if and so long as the new tenancy is an assured tenancy, it shall be an assured shorthold tenancy, whether or not it fulfils the conditions in paragraphs (a) to (c) of subsection (1) above.

(5) Subsection (4) above does not apply if, before the new tenancy is entered into (or, in the case of a statutory periodic tenancy, takes effect in possession), the landlord serves notice on the tenant that the new tenancy is not to be a shorthold tenancy.

(6) In the case of joint landlords—

(a) the reference in subsection (2)(c) above to the person who is to be the landlord is a reference to at least one of the persons who are to be joint landlords; and

(b) the reference in subsection (5) above to the landlord is a reference to at least one of the joint landlords.

(7) Section 14 above shall apply in relation to an assured shorthold tenancy as if in subsection (1) of that section the reference to an assured tenancy were a reference to an assured shorthold tenancy.

Recovery of possession on expiry or termination of assured shorthold tenancy

21.—(1) Without prejudice to any right of the landlord under an assured shorthold tenancy to recover possession of the dwelling-house let on the tenancy in accordance with Chapter I above, on or after the coming to an end of an assured shorthold tenancy which was a fixed term tenancy, a court shall make an order for possession of the dwelling-house if it is satisfied—

(a) that the assured shorthold tenancy has come to an end and no further assured tenancy (whether shorthold or not) is for the time being in existence, other than a statutory periodic tenancy; and

(b) the landlord or, in the case of joint landlords, at least one of them has given to the tenant not less than two months' notice stating that he requires possession of the dwelling-house.

(2) A notice under paragraph (b) of subsection (1) above may be given before or on the day on which the tenancy comes to an end; and that subsection shall have effect notwithstanding that on the coming to an end of the fixed term tenancy a statutory periodic tenancy arises.

(3) Where a court makes an order for possession of a dwelling-house by virtue of subsection (1) above, any statutory periodic tenancy which has arisen on the coming to an end of the assured shorthold tenancy shall end (without further notice and regardless of the period) on the day on which the order takes effect.

(4) Without prejudice to any such right as is referred to in subsection (1) above, a court shall make an order for possession of a dwelling-house let on an assured shorthold tenancy which is a periodic tenancy if the court is satisfied—

(a) that the landlord or, in the case of joint landlords, at least one of them has given to the tenant a notice stating that, after a date specified in the notice, being the last day of a period of the tenancy and not earlier than two months after the date the notice was given, possession of the dwelling-house is required by virtue of this section; and

(b) that the date specified in the notice under paragraph (a) above is not earlier than the earliest day on which, apart from section 5(1) above, the tenancy could be brought to an end by a notice to quit given by the landlord on the same date as the notice under paragraph (a) above.

Reference of excessive rents to rent assessment committee

22.—(1) Subject to section 23 and subsection (2) below, the tenant under an assured shorthold tenancy in respect of which a notice was served as mentioned in section 20(2) above may make an application in the prescribed form to a rent assessment committee for a determination of the rent which, in the committee's opinion, the landlord might reasonably be expected to obtain under the assured shorthold tenancy.

(2) No application may be made under this section if—

(a) the rent payable under the tenancy is a rent previously determined under this section; or

(b) the tenancy is an assured shorthold tenancy falling within subsection (4) of section 20 above (and, accordingly, is one in respect of which notice need not have been served as mentioned in subsection (2) of that section).

(3) Where an application is made to a rent assessment committee under subsection (1) above with respect to the rent under an assured shorthold tenancy, the committee shall not make such a determination as is referred to in that subsection unless they consider—

(a) that there is a sufficient number of similar dwelling-houses in the locality let on assured tenancies (whether shorthold or not); and

(b) that the rent payable under the assured shorthold tenancy in question is significantly higher than the rent which the landlord might reasonably be expected to be able to obtain under the tenancy, having regard to the level of rents payable under the tenancies referred to in paragraph (a) above.

(4) Where, on an application under this section, a rent assessment committee make a determination of a rent for an assured shorthold tenancy—

(a) the determination shall have effect from such date as the committee may direct, not being earlier than the date of the application;

(b) if, at any time on or after the determination takes effect, the rent which, apart from this paragraph, would be payable under the tenancy exceeds the rent so determined, the excess shall be irrecoverable from the tenant; and

(c) no notice may be served under section 13(2) above with respect to a tenancy of the dwelling-house in question until after the first anniversary of the date on which the determination takes effect.

(5) Subsections (4), (5) and (8) of section 14 above apply in relation to a determination of rent under this section as they apply in relation to a determination under that section and, accordingly, where subsection (5) of that section applies, any reference in subsection (4)(b) above to rent is a reference to rent exclusive of the amount attributable to rates.

Termination of rent assessment committee's functions
23.—(1) If the Secretary of State by order made by statutory instrument so provides, section 22 above shall not apply in such cases or to tenancies of dwelling-houses in such areas or in such other circumstances as may be specified in the order.

(2) An order under this section may contain such transitional, incidental and supplementary provisions as appear to the Secretary of State to be desirable.

(3) No order shall be made under this section unless a draft of the order has been laid before, and approved by a resolution of, each House of Parliament.

CHAPTER IV

PROTECTION FROM EVICTION

Damages for unlawful eviction
27.—(1) This section applies if, at any time after 9th June 1988, a landlord (in this section referred to as "the landlord in default") or any person acting on behalf of the landlord in default unlawfully deprives the residential occupier of any premises of his occupation of the whole or part of the premises.

(2) This section also applies if, at any time after 9th June 1988, a landlord (in this section referred to as "the landlord in default") or any person acting on behalf of the landlord in default—

(a) attempts unlawfully to deprive the residential occupier of any premises of his occupation of the whole or part of the premises, or

(b) knowing or having reasonable cause to believe that the conduct is likely to cause the residential occupier of any premises—

(i) to give up his occupation of the premises or any part thereof, or

(ii) to refrain from exercising any right or pursuing any remedy in respect of the premises or any part thereof,

does acts likely to interfere with the peace or comfort of the residential occupier or members of his household, or persistently withdraws or withholds services reasonably required for the occupation of the premises as a residence,

and, as a result, the residential occupier gives up his occupation of the premises as a residence.

(3) Subject to the following provisions of this section, where this section applies, the landlord in default shall, by virtue of this section, be liable to pay to the former residential occupier, in respect of his loss of the right to occupy the premises in question as his residence, damages assessed on the basis set out in section 28 below.

(4) Any liability arising by virtue of subsection (3) above—

(a) shall be in the nature of a liability in tort; and

(b) subject to subsection (5) below, shall be in addition to any liability arising apart from this section (whether in tort, contract or otherwise).

(5) Nothing in this section affects the right of a residential occupier to enforce any liability which arises apart from this section in respect of his loss of the right to occupy premises as his residence; but damages shall not be awarded both in respect of such a liability and in respect of a liability arising by virtue of this section on account of the same loss.

(6) No liability shall arise by virtue of subsection (3) above if—

(a) before the date on which proceedings to enforce the liability are finally disposed of, the former residential occupier is reinstated in the premises in question in such circumstances that he becomes again the residential occupier of them; or

(b) at the request of the former residential occupier, a court makes an order (whether in the nature of an injunction or otherwise) as a result of which he is reinstated as mentioned in paragraph (a) above;

and, for the purposes of paragraph (a) above, proceedings to enforce a liability are finally disposed of on the earliest date by which the proceedings (including any proceedings on or in consequence of an appeal) have been determined and any time for appealing or further appealing has expired, except that if any appeal is abandoned, the proceedings shall be taken to be disposed of on the date of the abandonment.

(7) If, in proceedings, to enforce a liability arising by virtue of subsection (3) above, it appears to the court—

(a) that, prior to the event which gave rise to the liability, the conduct of the former residential occupier or any person living with him in the premises concerned was such that it is reasonable to mitigate the damages for which the landlord in default would otherwise be liable, or

(b) that, before the proceedings were begun, the landlord in default offered to reinstate the former residential occupier in the premises in question and either it was unreasonable of the former residential occupier to refuse that offer or, if he had obtained alternative accommodation before the offer was made, it would have been unreasonable of him to refuse that offer if he had not obtained that accommodation,

the court may reduce the amount of damages which would otherwise be payable to such amount as it thinks appropriate.

(8) In proceedings to enforce a liability arising by virtue of subsection (3) above, it shall be a defence for the defendant to prove that he believed, and had reasonable cause to believe—

(a) that the residential occupier had ceased to reside in the premises in question at the time when he was deprived of occupation as mentioned in subsection (1) above or, as the case may be, when the attempt was made or the acts were done as a result of which he gave up his occupation of those premises; or

(b) that, where the liability would otherwise arise by virtue only of the doing of acts or the withdrawal or withholding of services, he had reasonable grounds for doing the acts or withdrawing or withholding the services in question.

(9) In this section—

(a) "residential occupier", in relation to any premises, has the same meaning as in section 1 of the 1977 Act;

(b) "the right to occupy", in relation to a residential occupier, includes any restriction on the right of another person to recover possession of the premises in question;

(c) "landlord", in relation to a residential occupier, means the person who, but for the occupier's right to occupy, would be entitled to occupation of the premises and any superior landlord under whom that person derives title;

(d) "former residential occupier", in relation to any premises, means the person who was the residential occupier until he was deprived of or gave up his occupation as mentioned in subsection (1) or subsection (2) above (and, in relation to a former residential occupier, "the right to occupy" and "landlord" shall be construed accordingly).

The measure of damages

28.—(1) The basis for the assessment of damages referred to in section 27(3) above is the difference in value, determined as at the time immediately before the residential occupier ceased to occupy the premises in question as his residence, between—

(a) the value of the interest of the landlord in default determined on the assumption that the residential occupier continues to have the same right to occupy the premises as before that time; and

(b) the value of that interest determined on the assumption that the residential occupier has ceased to have that right.

(2) In relation to any premises, any reference in this section to the interest of the landlord in default is a reference to his interest in the building in which the premises in question are comprised (whether or not that building contains any other premises) together with its curtilage.

(3) For the purposes of the valuations referred to in subsection (1) above, it shall be assumed—

(a) that the landlord in default is selling his interest on the open market to a willing buyer;

(b) that neither the residential occupier nor any member of his family wishes to buy; and

(c) that it is unlawful to carry out any substantial development of any of the land in which the landlord's interest subsists or to demolish the whole or part of any building on that land.

(4) In this section "the landlord in default" has the same meaning as in section 27 above and subsection (9) of that section applies in relation to this section as it applies in relation to that.

(5) Section 113 of the Housing Act 1985 (meaning of "members of a person's family") applies for the purposes of subsection (3)(b) above.

(6) The reference in subsection (3)(c) above to substantial development of any of the land in which the landlord's interest subsists is a reference to any development other than—

(a) development for which planning permission is granted by a general develop-ment order for the time being in force and which is carried out so as to comply with any condition or limitation subject to which planning permission is so granted; or

(b) a change of use resulting in the building referred to in subsection (2) above or any part of it being used as, or as part of, one or more dwelling-houses;

and in this subsection "general development order" has the same meaning as in section 43(3) of the Town and Country Planning Act 1971 and other expressions have the same meaning as in that Act.

Offences of harassment
29.—(1) In section 1 of the 1977 Act (unlawful eviction and harassment of occupier), with respect to acts done after the commencement of this Act, subsection (3) shall have effect with the substitution, for the word "calculated", of the word "likely".

(2) After that subsection there shall be inserted the following subsections—

"(3A) Subject to subsection (3B) below, the landlord of a residential occupier or an agent of the landlord shall be guilty of an offence if—

(a) he does acts likely to interfere with the peace or comfort of the residential occupier or members of his household, or

(b) he persistently withdraws or withholds services reasonably required for the occupation of the premises in question as a residence,

and (in either case) he knows, or has reasonable cause to believe, that that conduct is likely to cause the residential occupier to give up the occupation of the whole or part of the premises or to refrain from exercising any right or pursuing any remedy in respect of the whole or part of the premises.

(3B) A person shall not be guilty of an offence under subsection (3A) above if he proves that he had reasonable grounds for doing the acts or withdrawing or withholding the services in question.

(3C) In subsection (3A) above "landlord", in relation to a residential occupier of any premises, means the person who, but for—

(a) the residential occupier's right to remain in occupation of the premises, or

(b) a restriction on the person's right to recover possession of the premises, would be entitled to occupation of the premises and any superior landlord under whom that person derives title."

Variation of scope of 1977 ss. 3 and 4

30.—(1) In section 3 of the 1977 Act (prohibition of eviction without due process of law), in subsection (1) for the words "not a statutorily protected tenancy" there shall be substituted "neither a statutorily protected tenancy nor an excluded tenancy".

(2) After subsection (2A) of that section there shall be inserted the following subsections—

"(2B) Subsections (1) and (2) above apply in relation to any premises occupied as a dwelling under a licence, other than an excluded licence, as they apply in relation to premises let as a dwelling under a tenancy, and in those subsections the expressions "let" and "tenancy" shall be construed accordingly.

(2C) References in the preceding provisions of this section and section 4(2A) below to an excluded tenancy do not apply to—

(a) a tenancy entered into before the date on which the Housing Act 1988 came into force, or

(b) a tenancy entered into on or after that date but pursuant to a contract made before that date,

but, subject to that, "excluded tenancy" and "excluded licence" shall be construed in accordance with section 3A below."

(3) In section 4 of the 1977 Act (special provisions for agricultural employees) after subsection (2) there shall be inserted the following subsection—

"(2A) In accordance with section 3(2B) above, any reference in subsections (1) and (2) above to the tenant under the former tenancy includes a reference to the licensee under a licence (other than an excluded licence) which has come to an end (being a licence to occupy premises as a dwelling); and in the following provisions of this section the expressions "tenancy" and "rent" and any other expressions referable to a tenancy shall be construed accordingly."

Excluded tenancies and licences

31. After section 3 of the 1977 Act there shall be inserted the following section—

"**3A.**—(1) Any reference in this Act to an excluded tenancy or an excluded licence is a reference to a tenancy or licence which is excluded by virtue of any of the following provisions of this section.

(2) A tenancy or licence is excluded if—

(a) under its terms the occupier shares any accommodation with the landlord or licensor; and

(b) immediately before the tenancy or licence was granted and also at the time it comes to an end, the landlord or licensor occupied as his only or principal home premises of which the whole or part of the shared accommodation formed part.

(3) A tenancy or licence is also excluded if—

(a) under its terms the occupier shares any accommodation with a member of the family of the landlord or licensor;

(b) immediately before the tenancy or licence was granted and also at the time it comes to an end, the member of the family of the landlord or licensor occupied as his only or principal home premises of which the whole or part of the shared accommodation formed part; and

(c) immediately before the tenancy or licence was granted and also at the time it comes to an end, the landlord or licensor occupied as his only or principal home premises in the same building as the shared accommodation and that building is not a purpose-built block of flats.

(4) For the purposes of subsections (2) and (3) above, an occupier shares accommodation with another person if he has the use of it in common with that person (whether or not also in common with others) and any reference in those subsections to shared accommodation shall be construed accordingly, and if, in relation to any tenancy or licence, there is at any time more than one person who is the landlord or licensor, any reference in those subsections to the landlord or licensor shall be construed as a reference to any one of those persons.

(5) In subsections (2) to (4) above—

(a) "accommodation" includes neither an area used for storage nor a staircase, passage, corridor or other means of access;

(b) "occupier" means, in relation to a tenancy, the tenant and, in relation to a licence, the licensee; and

(c) "purpose-built block of flats" has the same meaning as in Part III of Schedule 1 to the Housing Act 1988;

and section 113 of the Housing Act 1985 shall apply to determine whether a person is for the purposes of subsection (3) above a member of another's family as it applies for the purposes of Part IV of that Act.

(6) A tenancy or licence is excluded if it was granted as a temporary expedient to a person who entered the premises in question or any other premises as a trespasser (whether or not, before the beginning of that tenancy or licence, another tenancy or licence to occupy the premises or any other premises had been granted to him).

(7) A tenancy or licence is excluded if—

(a) it confers on the tenant or licensee the right to occupy the premises for a holiday only; or

(b) it is granted otherwise than for money or money's worth.

(8) A licence is excluded if it confers rights of occupation in a hostel, within the meaning of the Housing Act 1985, which is provided by—

(a) the council of a county, district or London Borough, the Common Council of the City of London, the Council of the Isles of Scilly, the Inner London Education Authority, a joint authority within the meaning of the Local Government Act 1985 or a residuary body within the meaning of that Act;

(b) a development corporation within the meaning of the New Towns Act 1981;

(c) the Commission for the New Towns;

(d) an urban development corporation established by an order under section 135 of the Local Government, Planning and Land Act 1980;

(e) a housing action trust established under Part III of the Housing Act 1988;

(f) the Development Board for Rural Wales;

(g) the Housing Corporation or Housing for Wales;

(h) a housing trust which is a charity or a registered housing association, within the meaning of the Housing Associations Act 1985; or

(i) any other person who is, or who belongs to a class of person which is, specified in an order made by the Secretary of State.

(9) The power to make an order under subsection (8)(i) above shall be exercisable by statutory instrument which shall be subject to annulment in pursuance of a resolution of either House of Parliament."

Notice to quit etc.

32.—(1) In section 5 of the 1977 Act (validity of notices to quit) at the beginning of subsection (1) there shall be inserted the words "Subject to subsection (1B) below".

(2) After subsection (1) of that section there shall be inserted the following subsections—

"(1A) Subject to subsection (1B) below, no notice by a licensor or a licensee to determine a periodic licence to occupy premises as a dwelling (whether the licence was granted before or after the passing of this Act) shall be valid unless—

(a) it is in writing and contains such information as may be prescribed, and

(b) it is given not less than 4 weeks before the date on which it is to take effect.

(1B) Nothing in subsection (1) or subsection (1A) above applies to—

(a) premises let on an excluded tenancy which is entered into on or after the date on which the Housing Act 1988 came into force unless it is entered into pursuant to a contract made before that date; or

(b) premises occupied under an excluded licence."

Interpretation of Chapter IV and the 1977 Act

33.—(1) In this Chapter "the 1977 Act" means the Protection from Eviction Act 1977.

(2) In section 8 of the 1977 Act (interpretation) at the end of subsection (1) (statutory protected tenancy) there shall be inserted—

"(e) an assured tenancy or assured agricultural occupancy under Part I of the Housing Act 1988."

(3) At the end of that section there shall be added the following subsections—

"(4) In this Act "excluded tenancy" and "excluded licence" have the meaning assigned by section 3A of this Act.

(5) If, on or after the date on which the Housing Act 1988 came into force,

the terms of an excluded tenancy or excluded licence entered into before that date are varied, then—

(a) If the variation affects the amount of the rent which is payable under the tenancy or licence, the tenancy or licence shall be treated for the purposes of sections 3(2C) and 5(1B) above as a new tenancy or licence entered into at the time of the variation; and

(b) if the variation does not affect the amount of the rent which is so payable, nothing in this Act shall affect the determination of the question whether the variation is such as to give rise to a new tenancy or licence.

(6) Any reference in subsection (5) above to a variation affecting the amount of the rent which is payable under a tenancy or licence does not include a reference to—

(a) a reduction or increase effected under Part III or Part VI of the Rent Act 1977 (rents under regulated tenancies and housing association tenancies), section 78 of that Act (power of rent tribunal in relation to restricted contracts) or sections 11 to 14 of the Rent (Agriculture) Act 1976; or

(b) a variation which is made by the parties and has the effect of making the rent expressed to be payable under the tenancy or licence the same as a rent for the dwelling which is entered in the register under Part IV or section 79 of the Rent Act 1977."

CHAPTER V

PHASING OUT OF RENT ACTS AND OTHER TRANSITIONAL PROVISIONS

New protected tenancies and agricultural occupanies restricted to special cases
34.—(1) A tenancy which is entered into on or after the commencement of this Act cannot be a protected tenancy, unless—

(a) it is entered into in pursuance of a contract made before the commencement of this Act; or

(b) it is granted to a person (alone or jointly with others) who, immediately before the tenancy was granted, was a protected or statutory tenant and is so granted by the person who at that time was the landlord (or one of the joint landlords) under the protected or statutory tenancy; or

(c) it is granted to a person (alone or jointly with others) in the following circumstances—

(i) prior to the grant of the tenancy, an order for possession of a dwelling-house was made against him (alone or jointly with others) on the court being satisfied as mentioned in section 98(1)(a) of, or Case 1 in Schedule 16 to, the Rent Act 1977 or Case 1 in Schedule 4 to the Rent (Agriculture) Act 1976 (suitable alternative accommodation available); and

(ii) the tenancy is of the premises which constitute the suitable alternative accommodation as to which the court was so satisfied; and

(iii) in the proceedings for possession the court considered that, in the circumstances, the grant of an assured tenancy would not afford the required security and, accordingly, directed that the tenancy would be a protected tenancy; or

(d) it is a tenancy in relation to which subsections (1) and (3) of section 38 below have effect in accordance with subsection (4) of that section.

(2) In subsection (1)(b) above "protected tenant" and "statutory tenant" do not include—

(a) a tenant under a protected shorthold tenancy;

(b) a protected or statutory tenant of a dwelling-house which was let under a protected shorthold tenancy which ended before the commencement of this Act and in respect of which at that commencement either there has been no grant of a further tenancy or any grant of a further tenancy has been to the person who, immediately before the grant, was in possession of the dwelling-house as a protected or statutory tenant;

and in this subsection "protected shorthold tenancy" includes a tenancy which, in proceedings for possession under Case 19 in Schedule 15 to the Rent Act 1977, is treated as a protected shorthold tenancy.

(3) In any case where—

(a) by virtue of subsections (1) and (2) above, a tenancy entered into on or after the commencement of this Act is an assured tenancy, but

(b) apart from subsection (2) above, the effect of subsection (1)(b) above would be that the tenancy would be a protected tenancy, and

(c) the landlord and the tenant under the tenancy are the same as at the coming to an end of the protected or statutory tenancy which, apart from subsection (2) above, would fall within subsection (1)(b) above,

the tenancy shall be an assured shorthold tenancy (whether or not it fulfils the conditions in section 20(1) above) unless, before the tenancy is entered into, the landlord serves notice on the tenant that it is not to be a shorthold tenancy.

(4) A licence or tenancy which is entered into on or after the commencement of this Act cannot be a relevant licence or relevant tenancy for the purposes of the Rent (Agriculture) Act 1976 (in this subsection referred to as "the 1976 Act") unless—

(a) it is entered into in pursuance of a contract made before the commencement of this Act; or

(b) it is granted to a person (alone or jointly with others) who, immediately before the licence or tenancy was granted, was a protected occupier or statutory tenant, within the meaning of the 1976 Act, and is so granted by the person who at that time was the landlord or licensor (or one of the joint landlords or licensors) under the protected occupancy or statutory tenancy in question.

(5) Except as provided in subsection (4) above, expressions used in this section have the same meaning as in the Rent Act 1977.

Removal of special regimes for tenancies of housing associations etc.

35.—(1) In this section "housing association tenancy" has the same meaning as in Part VI of the Rent Act 1977.

(2) A tenancy which is entered into on or after the commencement of this Act cannot be a housing association tenancy unless—

(a) it is entered into in pursuance of a contract made before the commencement of this Act; or

(b) it is granted to a person (alone or jointly with others) who, immediately before the tenancy was granted, was a tenant under a housing association tenancy and is so granted by the person who at that time was the landlord under that housing association tenancy; or

(c) it is granted to a person (alone or jointly with others) in the following circumstances—

(i) prior to the grant of the tenancy, an order for possession of a dwelling-house was made against him (alone or jointly with others) on the court being satisfied as mentioned in paragraph (b) or paragraph (c) of subsection (2) of section 84 of the Housing Act 1985; and

(ii) the tenancy is of the premises which constitute the suitable accommodation as to which the court was so satisfied; and

(iii) in the proceedings for possession the court directed that the tenancy would be a housing association tenancy; or

(d) it is a tenancy in relation to which subsections (1) and (3) of section 38 below have effect in accordance with subsection (4) of that section.

(3) Where, on or after the commencement of this Act, a registered housing association, within the meaning of the Housing Associations Act 1985, grants a secure tenancy pursuant to an obligation under section 554(2A) of the Housing Act 1985 (as set out in Schedule 17 to this Act) then, in determining whether that tenancy is a housing association tenancy, it shall be assumed for the purposes only of section 86(2)(b) of the Rent Act 1977 (tenancy would be a protected tenancy but for section 15 or 16 of that Act) that the tenancy was granted before the commencement of this Act.

(4) A tenancy or licence which is entered into on or after the commencement of this Act cannot be a secure tenancy unless—

(a) the interest of the landlord belongs to a local authority, a new town corporation or an urban development corporation, all within the meaning of section 80 of the Housing Act 1985, a housing action trust established under Part III of this Act or the Development Board for Rural Wales; or

(b) the interest of the landlord belongs to a housing co-operative within the meaning of section 27B of the Housing Act 1985 (agreements between local housing authorities and housing co-operatives) and the tenancy or licence is of a dwelling-house comprised in a housing co-operative agreement falling within that section; or

(c) it is entered into in pursuance of a contract made before the commencement of this Act; or

(d) it is granted to a person (alone or jointly with others) who, immediately before it was entered into, was a secure tenant and is so granted by the body which at that time was the landlord or licensor under the secure tenancy; or

(e) it is granted to a person (alone or jointly with others) in the following circumstances—

(i) prior to the grant of the tenancy or licence, an order for possession of a dwelling-house was made against him (alone or jointly with others) on the court being satisfied as mentioned in paragraph (b) or paragraph (c) of subsection (2) of section 84 of the Housing Act 1985; and

(ii) the tenancy or licence is of the premises which constitute the suitable accommodation as to which the court was so satisfied; and

(iii) in the proceedings for possession the court considered that, in the circumstances, the grant of an assured tenancy would not afford the required security and, accordingly, directed that the tenancy or licence would be a secure tenancy; or

(f) it is granted pursuant to an obligation under section 554(2A) of the Housing Act 1985 (as set out in Schedule 17 to this Act).

(5) If, on or after the commencement of this Act, the interest of the landlord under a protected or statutory tenancy becomes held by a housing association, a housing trust, the Housing Corporation or Housing for Wales, nothing in the preceding provisions of this section shall prevent the tenancy from being a housing association tenancy or a secure tenancy and, accordingly, in such a case section 80 of the Housing Act 1985 (and any enactment which refers to that section) shall have effect without regard to the repeal of provisions of that section effected by this Act.

(6) In subsection (5) above "housing association" and "housing trust" have the same meaning as in the Housing Act 1985.

New restricted contracts limited to transitional cases
36.—(1) A tenancy or other contract entered into after the commencement of this Act cannot be a restricted contract for the purposes of the Rent Act 1977 unless it is entered into in pursuance of a contract made before the commencement of this Act.

(2) If the terms of a restricted contract are varied after this Act comes into force then, subject to subsection (3) below,—

(a) if the variation affects the amount of the rent which, under the contract, is payable for the dwelling in question, the contract shall be treated as a new contract entered into at the time of the variation (and subsection (1) above shall have effect accordingly); and

(b) if the variation does not affect the amount of the rent which, under the contract, is so payable, nothing in this section shall affect the determination of the question whether the variation is such as to give rise to a new contract.

(3) Any reference in subsection (2) above to a variation affecting the amount of the rent which, under a contract, is payable for a dwelling does not include a reference to—

(a) a reduction or increase effected under section 78 of the Rent Act 1977 (power of rent tribunal); or

(b) a variation which is made by the parties and has the effect of making the rent expressed to be payable under the contract the same as the rent for the dwelling which is entered in the register under section 79 of the Rent Act 1977.

(4) In subsection (1) of section 81A of the Rent Act 1977 (cancellation of registration of rent relating to a restricted contract) paragraph (a) (no cancellation until two years have elapsed since the date of the entry) shall cease to have effect.

(5) In this section "rent" has the same meaning as in Part V of the Rent Act 1977.

No further assured tenancies under Housing Act 1980
37.—(1) A tenancy which is entered into on or after the commencement of this Act cannot be an assured tenancy for the purposes of sections 56 to 58 of the Housing Act 1980 (in this section referred to as a "1980 Act tenancy").

(2) In any case where—

(a) before the commencement of this Act, a tenant under a 1980 Act tenancy made an application to the court under section 24 of the Landlord and Tenant Act 1954 (for the grant of a new tenancy), and

(b) at the commencement of this Act the 1980 Act tenancy is continuing by virtue of that section or of any provision of Part IV of the said Act of 1954,

section 1(3) of this Act shall not apply to the 1980 Act tenancy.

(3) If, in a case falling within subsection (2) above, the court makes an order for the grant of a new tenancy under section 29 of the Landlord and Tenant Act 1954, that tenancy shall be an assured tenancy for the purposes of this Act.

(4) In any case where—

(a) before the commencement of this Act a contract was entered into for the grant of a 1980 Act tenancy, but

(b) at the commencement of this Act the tenancy had not been granted,

the contract shall have effect as a contract for the grant of an assured tenancy (within the meaning of this Act).

(5) In relation to an assured tenancy falling within subsection (3) above or granted pursuant to a contract falling within subsection (4) above, Part I of Schedule 1 to this Act shall have effect as if it consisted only of paragraphs 11 and 12; and, if the landlord granting the tenancy is a fully mutual housing association, then, so long as that association remains the landlord under that tenancy (and under any statutory periodic tenancy which arises on the coming to an end of that tenancy), the said paragraph 12 shall have effect in relation to that tenancy with the omission of sub-paragraph (1)(h).

(6) Any reference in this section to a provision of the Landlord and Tenant Act 1954 is a reference only to that provision as applied by section 58 of the Housing Act 1980.

Transfer of existing tenancies from public to private sector
38.—(1) The provisions of subsection (3) below apply in relation to a tenancy which was entered into before, or pursuant to a contract made before, the commencement of this Act if,—

(a) at that commencement or, if it is later, at the time it is entered into, the interest of the landlord is held by a public body (within the meaning of subsection (5) below); and

(b) at some time after that commencement, the interest of the landlord ceases to be so held.

(2) The provisions of subsection (3) below also apply in relation to a tenancy which was entered into before, or pursuant to a contract made before, the commencement of this Act if,—

(a) at the commencement of this Act or, if it is later, at the time it is entered into, it is a housing association tenancy; and

(b) at some time after that commencement, it ceases to be such a tenancy.

(3) On and after the time referred to in subsection (1)(b) or, as the case may be, subsection (2)(b) above—

(a) the tenancy shall not be capable of being a protected tenancy, a protected occupancy or a housing association tenancy;

(b) the tenancy shall not be capable of being a secure tenancy unless (and only at a time when) the interest of the landlord under the tenancy is (or is again) held by a public body; and

(c) paragraph 1 of Schedule 1 to this Act shall not apply in relation to it, and the question whether at any time thereafter it becomes (or remains) an assured tenancy shall be determined accordingly.

(4) In relation to a tenancy under which, at the commencement of this Act or, if it is later, at the time the tenancy is entered into, the interest of the landlord is held by a new town corporation, within the meaning of section 80 of the Housing Act 1985, subsections (1) and (3) above shall have effect as if any reference in subsection (1) above to the commencement of this Act were a reference to—

(a) the date on which expires the period of two years beginning on the day this Act is passed; or

(b) if the Secretary of State by order made by statutory instrument within that period so provides, such other date (whether earlier or later) as may be specified by the order for the purposes of this subsection.

(5) For the purposes of this section, the interest of a landlord under a tenancy is held by a public body at a time when—

(a) it belongs to a local authority, a new town corporation or an urban development corporation, all within the meaning of section 80 of the Housing Act 1985; or

(b) it belongs to a housing action trust established under Part III of this Act; or

(c) it belongs to the Development Board for Rural Wales; or

(d) it belongs to Her Majesty in right of the Crown or to a government department or is held in trust for Her Majesty for the purposes of a government department.

(6) In this section—

(a) "housing association tenancy" means a tenancy to which Part VI of the Rent Act 1977 applies;

(b) "protected tenancy" has the same meaning as in that Act; and

(c) "protected occupancy" has the same meaning as in the Rent (Agriculture) Act 1976.

Statutory tenants: succession
39.—(1) In section 2(1)(b) of the Rent Act 1977 (which introduces the provisions of Part I of Schedule 1 to that Act relating to statutory tenants by succession) after the words "statutory tenant of a dwelling-house" there shall be inserted "or, as the case may be, is entitled to an assured tenancy of a dwelling-house by succession".

(2) Where the person who is the original tenant, within the meaning of Part I of Schedule 1 to the Rent Act 1977, dies after the commencement of this Act, that Part shall have effect subject to the amendments in Part I of Schedule 4 to this Act.

(3) Where subsection (2) above does not apply but the person who is the first successor, within the meaning of Part I of Schedule 1 to the Rent Act 1977, dies after the commencement of this Act, that Part shall have effect subject to the amendments in paragraphs 5 to 9 of Part I of Schedule 4 to this Act.

(4) In any case where the original occupier, within the meaning of section 4 of the Rent (Agriculture) Act 1976 (statutory tenants and tenancies) dies after the commencement of

this Act, that section shall have effect subject to the amendments in Part II of Schedule 4 to this Act.

(5) In any case where, by virtue of any provision of—

(a) Part I of Schedule 1 to the Rent Act 1977, as amended in accordance with subsection (2) or subsection (3) above, or

(b) section 4 of the Rent (Agriculture) Act 1976, as amended in accordance with subsection (4) above,

a person (in the following provisions of this section referred to as "the successor") becomes entitled to an assured tenancy of a dwelling-house by succession, that tenancy shall be a periodic tenancy arising by virtue of this section.

(6) Where, by virtue of subsection (5) above, the successor becomes entitled to an assured periodic tenancy, that tenancy is one—

(a) taking effect in possession immediately after the death of the protected or statutory tenant or protected occupier (in the following provisions of this section referred to as "the predecessor") on whose death the successor became so entitled;

(b) deemed to have been granted to the successor by the person who, immediately before the death of the predecessor, was the landlord of the predecessor under his tenancy;

(c) under which the premises which are let are the same dwelling-house as, immediately before his death, the predecessor occupied under his tenancy;

(d) under which the periods of the tenancy are the same as those for which rent was last payable by the predecessor under his tenancy;

(e) under which, subject to sections 13 to 15 above, the other terms are the same as those on which, under his tenancy, the predecessor occupied the dwelling-house immediately before his death; and

(f) which, for the purposes of section 13(2) above, is treated as a statutory periodic tenancy;

and in paragraphs (b) to (e) above "under his tenancy", in relation to the predecessor, means under his protected tenancy or protected occupancy or in his capacity as a statutory tenant.

(7) If, immediately before the death of the predecessor, the landlord might have recovered possession of the dwelling-house under Case 19 in Schedule 15 to the Rent Act 1977, the assured periodic tenancy to which the successor becomes entitled shall be an assured shorthold tenancy (whether or not it fulfils the conditions in section 20(1) above).

(8) If, immediately before his death, the predecessor was a protected occupier or statutory tenant within the meaning of the Rent (Agriculture) Act 1976, the assured periodic tenancy to which the successor becomes entitled shall be an assured agricultural occupancy (whether or not it fulfils the conditions in section 24(1) above).

(9) Where, immediately before his death, the predecessor was a tenant under a fixed term tenancy, section 6 above shall apply in relation to the assured periodic tenancy to which the successor becomes entitled on the predecessor's death subject to the following modifications—

(a) for any reference to a statutory periodic tenancy there shall be substituted a reference to the assured periodic tenancy to which the successor becomes so entitled;

(b) in subsection (1) of that section, paragraph (a) shall be omitted and the reference in paragraph (b) to section 5(3)(e) above shall be construed as a reference to subsection (6)(e) above; and

(c) for any reference to the coming to an end of the former tenancy there shall be substituted a reference to the date of the predecessor's death.

(10) If and so long as a dwelling-house is subject to an assured tenancy to which the successor has become entitled by succession, section 7 above and Schedule 2 to this Act shall have effect subject to the modifications in Part III of Schedule 4 to this Act; and in that Part "the predecessor" and "the successor" have the same meaning as in this section.

CHAPTER VI

GENERAL PROVISIONS

Jurisdiction of county courts
40.—(1) A county court shall have jurisdiction to hear and determine any question arising under any provision of—

(a) Chapters I to III and V above, or

(b) sections 27 and 28 above,

other than a question falling within the jurisdiction of a rent assessment committee by virtue of any such provision.

(2) Subsection (1) above has effect notwithstanding that the damages claimed in any proceedings may exceed the amount which, for the time being, is the county court limit for the purposes of the County Courts Act 1984.

(3) Where any proceedings under any provision mentioned in subsection (1) above are being taken in a county court, the court shall have jurisdiction to hear and determine any other proceedings joined with those proceedings, notwithstanding that, apart from this subsection, those other proceedings would be outside the court's jurisdiction.

(4) If any person takes any proceedings under any provision mentioned in subsection (1) above in the High Court, he shall not be entitled to recover any more costs of those proceedings than those to which he would have been entitled if the proceedings had been taken in a county court: and in such a case the taxing master shall have the same power of directing on what county court scale costs are to be allowed, and of allowing any item of costs, as the judge would have had if the proceedings had been taken in a county court.

(5) Subsection (4) above shall not apply where the purpose of taking the proceedings in the High Court was to enable them to be joined with any proceedings already pending before that court (not being proceedings taken under any provision mentioned in subsection (1) above).

Rent assessment committees: procedure and information powers
41.—(1) In section 74 of the Rent Act 1977 (regulations made by the Secretary of State) at the end of paragraph (b) of subsection (1) (procedure of rent officers and rent assessment committees) there shall be added the words "whether under this Act or Part I of the Housing Act 1988".

(2) The rent assessment committee to whom a matter is referred under Chapter I or Chapter II above may by notice in the prescribed form served on the landlord or the tenant require him to give to the committee, within such period of not less than fourteen

days from the service of the notice as may be specified in the notice, such information as they may reasonably require for the purposes of their functions.

(3) If any person fails without reasonable excuse to comply with a notice served on him under subsection (2) above, he shall be liable on summary conviction to a fine not exceeding level 3 on the standard scale.

(4) Where an offence under subsection (3) above committed by a body corporate is proved to have been committed with the consent or connivance of, or to be attributable to any neglect on the part of, any director, manager or secretary or other similar officer of the body corporate or any person who was purporting to act in any such capacity, he as well as the body corporate shall be guilty of that offence and shall be liable to be proceeded against and punished accordingly.

Information as to determinations of rents
42.—(1) The President of every rent assessment panel shall keep and make publicly available, in such manner as is specified in an order made by the Secretary of State, such information as may be so specified with respect to rents under assured tenancies and assured agricultural occupancies which have been the subject of references or applications to, or determinations by, rent assessment committees.

(2) A copy of any information certified under the hand of an officer duly authorised by the President of the rent assessment panel concerned shall be receivable in evidence in any court and in any proceedings.

(3) An order under subsection (1) above—

(a) may prescribe the fees to be charged for the supply of a copy, including a certified copy, of any of the information kept by virtue of that subsection; and

(b) may make different provision with respect to different cases or descriptions of case, including different provision for different areas.

(4) The power to make an order under subsection (1) above shall be exercisable by statutory instrument which shall be subject to annulment in pursuance of a resolution of either House of Parliament.

Powers of local authorities for purposes of giving information
43. In section 149 of the Rent Act 1977 (which, among other matters, authorises local authorities to publish information for the benefit of landlords and tenants with respect to their rights and duties under certain enactments), in subsection (1)(a) after sub-paragraph (iv) there shall be inserted—

"(v) Chapters I to III of Part I of the Housing Act 1988".

Application to Crown Property
44.—(1) Subject to paragraph 11 of Schedule 1 to this Act and subsection (2) below, Chapters I to IV above apply in relation to premises in which there subsists, or at any material time subsisted, a Crown interest as they apply in relation to premises in relation to which no such interest subsists or ever subsisted.

(2) In Chapter IV above—

(a) sections 27 and 28 do not bind the Crown; and

(b) the remainder binds the Crown to the extent provided for in section 10 of the Protection from Eviction Act 1977.

(3) In this section "Crown interest" means an interest which belongs to Her Majesty

in right of the Crown or of the Duchy of Lancaster or to the Duchy of Cornwall, or to a government department, or which is held in trust for Her Majesty for the purposes of a government department.

(4) Where an interest belongs to Her Majesty in right of the Duchy of Lancaster, then, for the purposes of Chapters I to IV above, the Chancellor of the Duchy of Lancaster shall be deemed to be the owner of the interest.

Interpretation of Part I

45.—(1) In this Part of this Act, except where the context otherwise requires,—

"dwelling-house" may be a house or part of a house;

"fixed term tenancy" means any tenancy other than a periodic tenancy;

"fully mutual housing association" has the same meaning as in Part I of the Housing Associations Act 1985;

"landlord" includes any person from time to time deriving title under the original landlord and also includes, in relation to a dwelling-house, any person other than a tenant who is, or but for the existence of an assured tenancy would be, entitled to possession of the dwelling-house;

"let" includes "sub-let";

"prescribed" means prescribed by regulations made by the Secretary of State by statutory instrument;

"rates" includes water rates and charges but does not include an owner's drainage rate, as defined in section 63(2)(a) of the Land Drainage Act 1976;

"secure tenancy" has the meaning assigned by section 79 of the Housing Act 1985;

"statutory periodic tenancy" has the meaning assigned by section 5(7) above;

"tenancy" includes a sub-tenancy and an agreement for a tenancy or sub-tenancy; and

"tenant" includes a sub-tenant and any person deriving title under the original tenant or sub-tenant.

(2) Subject to paragraph 11 of Schedule 2 to this Act, any reference in this Part of this Act to the beginning of a tenancy is a reference to the day on which the tenancy is entered into or, if it is later, the day on which, under the terms of any lease, agreement or other document, the tenant is entitled to possession under the tenancy.

(3) Where two or more persons jointly constitute either the landlord or the tenant in relation to a tenancy, then, except where this Part of this Act otherwise provides, any reference to the landlord or to the tenant is a reference to all the persons who jointly constitute the landlord or the tenant, as the case may require.

(4) For the avoidance of doubt, it is hereby declared that any reference in this Part of this Act (however expressed) to a power for a landlord to determine a tenancy does not include a reference to a power of re-entry or forfeiture for breach of any term or condition of the tenancy.

(5) Regulations under subsection (1) above may make different provision with respect to different cases or descriptions of case, including different provision for different areas.

PART V

MISCELLANEOUS AND GENERAL

Leases

Premiums on long leases
115.—(1) With respect to—

(a) any premium received or required to be paid after the commencement of this Act, or

(b) any loan required to be made after that commencement,

section 127 of the Rent Act 1977 (allowable premiums in relation to certain long tenancies) shall have effect subject to the amendments in subsections (2) and (3) below.

(2) For subsections (2) and (3) there shall be substituted the following subsections—

"(2) The conditions mentioned in subsection (1)(a) above are—

(a) that the landlord has no power to determine the tenancy at any time within twenty years beginning on the date when it was granted; and

(b) that the terms of the tenancy do not inhibit both the assignment and the underletting of the whole of the premises comprised in the tenancy;

but for the purpose of paragraph (b) above there shall be disregarded any term of the tenancy which inhibits assignment and underletting only during a period which is or falls within the final seven years of the term for which the tenancy was granted.

(3) The reference in subsection (2) above to a power of the landlord to determine a tenancy does not include a reference to a power of re-entry or forfeiture for breach of any term or condition of the tenancy."

(3) Subsections (3C) and (3D) shall be omitted and in subsection (5) for "(2)(c)" there shall be substituted "(2)(b)".

(4) Expressions used in subsection (1) above have the same meaning as in Part IX of the Rent Act 1977.

Repairing obligations in short leases
116.—(1) In section 11 of the Landlord and Tenant Act 1985 (repairing obligations in short leases) after subsection (1) there shall be inserted the following subsections—

"(1A) If a lease to which this section applies is a lease of a dwelling-house which forms part only of a building, then, subject to subsection (1B), the covenant implied by subsection (1) shall have effect as if—

(a) the reference in paragraph (a) of that subsection to the dwelling-house included a reference to any part of the building in which the lessor has an estate or interest; and

(b) any reference in paragraphs (b) and (c) of that subsection to an installation in the dwelling-house included a reference to an installation which, directly or indirectly, serves the dwelling-house and which either—

(i) forms part of any part of a building in which the lessor has an estate or interest; or

(ii) is owned by the lessor or under his control.

(1B) Nothing in subsection (1A) shall be construed as requiring the lessor to carry out any works or repairs unless the disrepair (or failure to maintain in working order) is such as to affect the lessee's enjoyment of the dwelling-house or of any common parts, as defined in section 60(1) of the Landlord and Tenant Act 1987, which the lessee, as such, is entitled to use."

(2) After subsection (3) of that section there shall be inserted the following subsection—

"(3A) In any case where—

(a) the lessor's repairing covenant has effect as mentioned in subsection (1A), and

(b) in order to comply with the covenant the lessor needs to carry out works or repairs otherwise than in, or to an installation in, the dwelling-house, and

(c) the lessor does not have a sufficient right in the part of the building or the installation concerned to enable him to carry out the required works or repairs,

then, in any proceedings relating to a failure to comply with the lessor's repairing covenant, so far as it requires the lessor to carry out the works or repairs in question, it shall be a defence for the lessor to prove that he used all reasonable endeavours to obtain, but was unable to obtain, such rights as would be adequate to enable him to carry out the works or repairs."

(3) At the end of section 14(4) of the said Act of 1985 (which excludes from section 11 certain leases granted to various bodies) there shall be added—

"a housing action trust established under Part III of the Housing Act 1988".

(4) The amendments made by this section do not have effect with respect to—

(a) a lease entered into before the commencement of this Act; or

(b) a lease entered into pursuant to a contract made before the commencement of this Act.

Amendment of Landlord and Tenant Act 1987
119. The Landlord and Tenant Act 1987 shall have effect subject to the amendments in Schedule 13 to this Act.

Rent officers

Appointment etc. of rent officers
120. Section 63 of the Rent Act 1977 (schemes for the appointment of rent officers) shall have effect subject to the amendments in Part I of Schedule 14 to this Act and after section 64 of that Act there shall be inserted the sections set out in Part II of that Schedule.

Rent officers: additional functions relating to housing benefit etc.
121.—(1) The Secretary of State may by order require rent officers to carry out such functions as may be specified in the order in connection with housing benefit and rent allowance subsidy.

(2) An order under this section—

(a) shall be made by statutory instrument which, except in the case of the first order to be made, shall be subject to annulment in pursuance of a resolution of either House of Parliament;

(b) may make different provision for different cases or classes of case and for different areas; and

(c) may contain such transitional, incidental and supplementary provisions as appear to the Secretary of State to be desirable;

and the first order under this section shall not be made unless a draft of it has been laid before, and approved by a resolution of, each House of Parliament.

(3) In subsection (7) of section 63 of the Rent Act 1977 (expenditure arising in connection with rent officers etc.), in paragraph (a) after the words "this section" there shall be inserted "or an order under section 121 of the Housing Act 1988".

(4) At the end of section 21(6) of the Social Security Act 1986 (regulations prescribing maximum family credit and maximum housing benefit) there shall be added the words "and regulations prescribing the appropriate maximum housing benefit may provide for benefit to be limited by reference to determinations made by rent officers in exercise of functions conferred under section 121 of the Housing Act 1988".

(5) In section 30 of that Act (housing benefit finance) at the end of subsection (2) there shall be added the words "and, in relation to rent allowance subsidy, the Secretary of State may exercise his discretion as to what is unreasonable for the purposes of paragraph (b) above by reference to determinations made by rent officers in exercise of functions conferred under section 121 of the Housing Act 1988".

(6) In section 51(1)(h) of that Act (regulations may require information etc. needed for determination of a claim) the reference to information or evidence needed for the determination of a claim includes a reference to information or evidence required by a rent officer for the purpose of a function conferred on him under this section.

(7) In this section "housing benefit" and "rent allowance subsidy" have the same meaning as in Part II of the Social Security Act 1986.

SCHEDULES

SCHEDULE 1

Tenancies Which Cannot be Assured Tenancies

Part I

The Tenancies

Tenancies entered into before commencement

1. A tenancy which is entered into before, or pursuant to a contract made before, the commencement of this Act.

Tenancies of dwelling-houses with high rateable values

2. A tenancy under which the dwelling-house has for the time being a rateable value which,—

(a) if it is in Greater London, exceeds £1,500; and

(b) if it is elsewhere, exceeds £750.

Tenancies at a low rent

3.—(1) A tenancy under which either no rent is payable or the rent payable is less than two-thirds of the rateable value of the dwelling-house for the time being.

(2) In determining whether the rent under a tenancy falls within sub-paragraph (1) above, there shall be disregarded such part (if any) of the sums payable by the tenant as is expressed (in whatever terms) to be payable in respect of rates, services, management, repairs, maintenance or insurance, unless it could not have been regarded by the parties to the tenancy as a part so payable.

Business tenancies

4. A tenancy to which Part II of the Landlord and Tenant Act 1954 applies (business tenancies).

Licensed premises

5. A tenancy under which the dwelling-house consists of or comprises premises licensed for the sale of intoxicating liquors for consumption on the premises.

Tenancies of agricultural land

6.—(1) A tenancy under which agricultural land, exceeding two acres, is let together with the dwelling-house.

(2) In this paragraph "agricultural land" has the meaning set out in section 26(3)(a) of the General Rate Act 1967 (exclusion of agricultural land and premises from liability for rating).

Tenancies of agricultural holdings

7. A tenancy under which the dwelling-house—

(a) is comprised in an agricultural holding (within the meaning of the Agricultural Holdings Act 1986); and

(b) is occupied by the person responsible for the control (whether as tenant or as servant or agent of the tenant) of the farming of the holding.

Lettings to students

8.—(1) A tenancy which is granted to a person who is pursuing, or intends to pursue, a course of study provided by a specified educational institution and is so granted either by that institution or by another specified institution or body of persons.

(2) In sub-paragraph (1) above "specified" means specified, or of a class specified, for the purposes of this paragraph by regulations made by the Secretary of State by statutory instrument.

(3) A statutory instrument made in the exercise of the power conferred by sub-paragraph (2) above shall be subject to annulment in pursuance of a resolution of either House of Parliament.

Holiday lettings

9. A tenancy the purpose of which is to confer on the tenant the right to occupy the dwelling-house for a holiday.

Resident landlords

10.—(1) A tenancy in respect of which the following conditions are fulfilled—

(a) that the dwelling-house forms part only of a building and, except in a case where the dwelling-house also forms part of a flat, the building is not a purpose-built block of flats; and

(b) that, subject to Part III of this Schedule, the tenancy was granted by an individual who, at the time when the tenancy was granted, occupied as his only or principal home another dwelling-house which,—

> (i) in the case mentioned in paragraph (a) above, also forms part of the flat; or

> (ii) in any other case, also forms part of the building; and

(c) that, subject to Part III of this Schedule, at all times since the tenancy was granted the interest of the landlord under the tenancy has belonged to an individual who, at the time he owned that interest, occupied as his only or principal home another dwelling-house which,—

> (i) in the case mentioned in paragraph (a) above, also formed part of the flat; or

> (ii) in any other case, also formed part of the building; and

(d) that the tenancy is not one which is excluded from this sub-paragraph by sub-paragraph (3) below.

(2) If a tenancy was granted by two or more persons jointly, the reference in sub-paragraph (1)(b) above to an individual is a reference to any one of those persons and if the interest of the landlord is for the time being held by two or more persons jointly, the reference in sub-paragraph (1)(c) above to an individual is a reference to any one of those persons.

(3) A tenancy (in this sub-paragraph referred to as "the new tenancy") is excluded from sub-paragraph (1) above if—

(a) it is granted to a person (alone, or jointly with others) who, immediately before it was granted, was a tenant under an assured tenancy (in this sub-paragraph referred to as "the former tenancy") of the same dwelling-house or of another dwelling-house which forms part of the building in question; and

(b) the landlord under the new tenancy and under the former tenancy is the same person or, if either of those tenancies is or was granted by two or more persons jointly, the same person is the landlord or one of the landlords under each tenancy.

Crown tenancies

11.—(1) A tenancy under which the interest of the landlord belongs to Her Majesty in right of the Crown or to a government department or is held in trust for Her Majesty for the purposes of a government department.

(2) The reference in sub-paragraph (1) above to the case where the interest of the landlord belongs to Her Majesty in right of the Crown does not include the case where that interest is under the management of the Crown Estate Commissioners.

Local authority tenancies etc.

12.—(1) A tenancy under which the interest of the landlord belongs to—

(a) a local authority, as defined in sub-paragraph (2) below;

(b) the Commission for the New Towns;

(c) the Development Board for Rural Wales;

(d) an urban development corporation established by an order under section 135 of the Local Government, Planning and Land Act 1980;

(e) a development corporation, within the meaning of the New Towns Act 1981;

(f) an authority established under section 10 of the Local Government Act 1985 (waste disposal authorities);

(g) a residuary body, within the meaning of the Local Government Act 1985;

(h) a fully mutual housing association; or

(i) a housing action trust established under Part III of this Act.

(2) The following are local authorities for the purposes of sub-paragraph (1)(a) above—

(a) the council of a county, district or London borough;

(b) the Common Council of the City of London;

(c) the Council of the Isles of Scilly;

(d) the Broads Authority;

(e) the Inner London Education Authority; and

(f) a joint authority, within the meaning of the Local Government Act 1985.

Transitional cases

13.—(1) A protected tenancy, within the meaning of the Rent Act 1977.

(2) A housing association tenancy, within the meaning of Part VI of that Act.

(3) A secure tenancy.

(4) Where a person is a protected occupier of a dwelling-house, within the meaning of the Rent (Agriculture) Act 1976, the relevant tenancy, within the meaning of that Act, by virtue of which he occupies the dwelling-house.

PART II

RATEABLE VALUES

14.—(1) The rateable value of a dwelling-house at any time shall be ascertained for the purposes of Part I of this Schedule as follows—

(a) if the dwelling-house is a hereditament for which a rateable value is then shown in the valuation list, it shall be that rateable value;

(b) if the dwelling-house forms part only of such a hereditament or consists of or forms part of more than one such hereditament, its rateable value shall be taken to be such value as is found by a proper apportionment or aggregation of the rateable value or values so shown.

(2) Any question arising under this Part of this Schedule as to the proper apportionment or aggregation of any value or values shall be determined by the county court and the decision of that court shall be final.

15. Where, after the time at which the rateable value of a dwelling-house is material

for the purposes of any provision of Part I of this Schedule, the valuation list is altered so as to vary the rateable value of the hereditament of which the dwelling-house consists (in whole or in part) or forms part and the alteration has effect from that time or from an earlier time, the rateable value of the dwelling-house at the material time shall be ascertained as if the value shown in the valuation list at the material time had been the value shown in the list as altered.

16. Paragraphs 14 and 15 above apply in relation to any other land which, under section 2 of this Act, is treated as part of a dwelling-house as they apply in relation to the dwelling-house itself.

PART III

PROVISIONS FOR DETERMINING APPLICATION OF PARAGRAPH 10 (RESIDENT LANDLORDS)

17.—(1) In determining whether the condition in paragraph 10(1)(c) above is at any time fulfilled with respect to a tenancy, there shall be disregarded—

(a) any period of not more than twenty-eight days, beginning with the date on which the interest of the landlord under the tenancy becomes vested at law and in equity in an individual who, during that period, does not occupy as his only or principal home another dwelling-house which forms part of the building or, as the case may be, flat concerned;

(b) if, within a period falling within paragraph (a) above, the individual concerned notifies the tenant in writing of his intention to occupy as his only or principal home another dwelling-house in the building or, as the case may be, flat concerned, the period beginning with the date on which the interest of the landlord under the tenancy becomes vested in that individual as mentioned in that paragraph and ending—

(i) at the expiry of the period of six months beginning on that date, or

(ii) on the date on which that interest ceases to be so vested, or

(iii) on the date on which that interest becomes again vested in such an individual as is mentioned in paragraph 10(1)(c) or the condition in that paragraph becomes deemed to be fulfilled by virtue of paragraph 18(1) or paragraph 20 below,

whichever is the earlier; and

(c) any period of not more than two years beginning with the date on which the interest of the landlord under the tenancy becomes, and during which it remains, vested—

(i) in trustees as such; or
(ii) by virtue of section 9 of the Administration of Estates Act 1925, in the Probate Judge, within the meaning of that Act.

(2) Where the interest of the landlord under a tenancy becomes vested at law and in equity in two or more persons jointly, of whom at least one was an individual, sub-paragraph (1) above shall have effect subject to the following modifications—

(a) in paragraph (a) for the words from "an individual" to "occupy" there shall be substituted "the joint landlords if, during that period none of them occupies"; and

(b) in paragraph (b) for the words "the individual concerned" there shall be substituted "any of the joint landlords who is an individual" and for the words "that individual" there shall be substituted "the joint landlords".

18.—(1) During any period when—

(a) the interest of the landlord under the tenancy referred to in paragraph 10 above is vested in trustees as such, and

(b) that interest is or, if it is held on trust for sale, the proceeds of its sale are held on trust for any person who or for two or more persons of whom at least one occupies as his only or principal home a dwelling-house which forms part of the building or, as the case may be, flat referred to in paragraph 10(1)(a),

the condition in paragraph 10(1)(c) shall be deemed to be fulfilled and accordingly, no part of that period shall be disregarded by virtue of paragraph 17 above.

(2) If a period during which the condition in paragraph 10(1)(c) is deemed to be fulfilled by virtue of sub-paragraph (1) above comes to an end on the death of a person who was in occupation of a dwelling-house as mentioned in paragraph (b) of that sub-paragraph, then, in determining whether that condition is at any time thereafter fulfilled, there shall be disregarded any period—

(a) which begins on the date of the death;

(b) during which the interest of the landlord remains vested as mentioned in sub-paragraph (1)(a) above; and

(c) which ends at the expiry of the period of two years beginning on the date of the death or on any earlier date on which the condition in paragraph 10(1)(c) becomes again deemed to be fulfilled by virtue of sub-paragraph (1) above.

19. In any case where—

(a) immediately before a tenancy comes to an end the condition in paragraph 10(1)(c) is deemed to be fulfilled by virtue of paragraph 18(1) above, and

(b) on the coming to an end of that tenancy the trustees in whom the interest of the landlord is vested grant a new tenancy of the same or substantially the same dwelling-house to a person (alone or jointly with others) who was the tenant or one of the tenants under the previous tenancy,

the condition in paragraph 10(1)(b) above shall be deemed to be fulfilled with respect to the new tenancy.

20.—(1) The tenancy referred to in paragraph 10 above falls within this paragraph if the interest of the landlord under the tenancy becomes vested in the personal representatives of a deceased person acting in that capacity.

(2) If the tenancy falls within this paragraph, the condition in paragraph 10(1)(c) shall be deemed to be fulfilled for any period, beginning with the date on which the interest becomes vested in the personal representatives and not exceeding two years, during which the interest of the landlord remains so vested.

21. Throughout any period which, by virtue of paragraph 17 or paragraph 18(2) above, falls to be disregarded for the purpose of determining whether the condition in paragraph 10(1)(c) is fulfilled with respect to a tenancy, no order shall be made for possession of the dwelling-house subject to that tenancy, other than an order which might be made if that tenancy were or, as the case may be, had been an assured tenancy.

22. For the purposes of paragraph 10 above, a building is a purpose-built block of flats

if as constructed it contained, and it contains, two or more flats; and for this purpose "flat" means a dwelling-house which—

(a) forms part only of a building; and

(b) is separated horizontally from another dwelling-house which forms part of the same building.

SCHEDULE 2

GROUNDS FOR POSSESSION OF DWELLING-HOUSES LET ON ASSURED TENANCIES

PART I

GROUNDS ON WHICH COURT MUST ORDER POSSESSION

Ground 1

Not later than the beginning of the tenancy the landlord gave notice in writing to the tenant that possession might be recovered on this ground or the court is of the opinion that it is just and equitable to dispense with the requirement of notice and (in either case)—

(a) at some time before the beginning of the tenancy, the landlord who is seeking possession or, in the case of joint landlords seeking possession, at least one of them occupied the dwelling-house as his only or principal home; or

(b) the landlord who is seeking possession or, in the case of joint landlords seeking possession, at least one of them requires the dwelling-house as his or his spouse's only or principal home and neither the landlord (or, in the case of joint landlords, any one of them) nor any other person who, as landlord, derived title under the landlord who gave the notice mentioned above acquired the reversion on the tenancy for money or money's worth.

Ground 2

The dwelling-house is subject to a mortgage granted before the beginning of the tenancy and—

(a) the mortgagee is entitled to exercise a power of sale conferred on him by the mortgage or by section 101 of the Law of Property Act 1925; and

(b) the mortgagee requires possession of the dwelling-house for the purpose of disposing of it with vacant possession in exercise of that power, and

(c) either notice was given as mentioned in Ground 1 above or the court is satisfied that it is just and equitable to dispense with the requirement of notice;

and for the purposes of this ground "mortgage" includes a charge and "mortgagee" shall be construed accordingly.

Ground 3

The tenancy is a fixed term tenancy for a term not exceeding eight months and—

(a) not later than the beginning of the tenancy the landlord gave notice in writing to the tenant that possession might be recovered on this ground; and

(b) at some time within the period of twelve months ending with the beginning of the tenancy, the dwelling-house was occupied under a right to occupy it for a holiday.

Ground 4

The tenancy is a fixed term tenancy for a term not exceeding twelve months and—

(a) not later than the beginning of the tenancy the landlord gave notice in writing to the tenant that possession might be recovered on this ground; and

(b) at some time within the period of twelve months ending with the beginning of the tenancy, the dwelling-house was let on a tenancy falling within paragraph 8 of Schedule 1 to this Act.

Ground 5

The dwelling-house is held for the purpose of being available for occupation by a minister of religion as a residence from which to perform the duties of his office and—

(a) not later than the beginning of the tenancy the landlord gave notice in writing to the tenant that possession might be recovered on this ground; and

(b) the court is satisfied that the dwelling-house is required for occupation by a minister of religion as such a residence.

Ground 6

The landlord who is seeking possession or, if that landlord is a registered housing association or charitable housing trust, a superior landlord intends to demolish or reconstruct the whole or a substantial part of the dwelling-house or to carry out substantial works on the dwelling-house or any part thereof or any building of which it forms part and the following conditions are fulfilled—

(a) the intended work cannot reasonably be carried out without the tenant giving up possession of the dwelling-house because—

(i) the tenant is not willing to agree to such a variation of the terms of the tenancy as would give such access and other facilities as would permit the intended work to be carried out, or

(ii) the nature of the intended work is such that no such variation is practicable, or

(iii) the tenant is not willing to accept an assured tenancy of such part only of the dwelling-house (in this sub-paragraph referred to as "the reduced part") as would leave in the possession of his landlord so much of the dwelling-house as would be reasonable to enable the intended work to be carried out and, where appropriate, as would give such access and other facilities over the reduced part as would permit the intended work to be carried out, or

(iv) the nature of the intended work is such that such a tenancy is not practicable; and

(b) either the landlord seeking possession acquired his interest in the dwelling-house before the grant of the tenancy or that interest was in existence at the time of that grant and neither that landlord (or, in the case of joint landlords, any of them) nor any other person who, alone or jointly with others, has acquired that interest since that time acquired it for money or money's worth; and

(c) the assured tenancy on which the dwelling-house is let did not come into being by virtue of any provision of Schedule 1 to the Rent Act 1977, as amended by Part I of Schedule 4 to this Act or, as the case may be, section 4 of the Rent (Agriculture) Act 1976, as amended by Part II of that Schedule.

For the purposes of this ground, if, immediately before the grant of the tenancy, the tenant to whom it was granted or, if it was granted to joint tenants, any of them was the tenant or one of the joint tenants under an earlier assured tenancy of the dwelling-house concerned, any reference in paragraph (b) above to the grant of the tenancy is a reference to the grant of that earlier assured tenancy.

For the purposes of this ground "registered housing association" has the same meaning as in the Housing Associations Act 1985 and "charitable housing trust" means a housing trust, within the meaning of that Act, which is a charity, within the meaning of the Charities Act 1960.

Ground 7

The tenancy is a periodic tenancy (including a statutory periodic tenancy) which has devolved under the will or intestacy of the former tenant and the proceedings for the recovery of possession are begun not later than twelve months after the death of the former tenant or, if the court so directs, after the date on which, in the opinion of the court, the landlord or, in the case of joint landlords, any one of them became aware of the former tenant's death.

For the purposes of this ground, the acceptance by the landlord of rent from a new tenant after the death of the former tenant shall not be regarded as creating a new periodic tenancy, unless the landlord agrees in writing to a change (as compared with the tenancy before the death) in the amount of the rent, the period of the tenancy, the premises which are let or any other term of the tenancy.

Ground 8

Both at the date of the service of the notice under section 8 of this Act relating to the proceedings for possession and at the date of the hearing—

(a) if rent is payable weekly or fortnightly, at least thirteen weeks' rent is unpaid;

(b) if rent is payable monthly, at least three months' rent is unpaid;

(c) if rent is payable quarterly, at least one quarter's rent is more than three months in arrears; and

(d) if rent is payable yearly, at least three months' rent is more than three months in arrears;

and for the purpose of this ground "rent" means rent lawfully due from the tenant.

PART II

GROUNDS ON WHICH COURT MAY ORDER POSSESSION

Ground 9

Suitable alternative accommodation is available for the tenant or will be available for him when the order for possession takes effect.

Ground 10

Some rent lawfully due from the tenant—

(a) is unpaid on the date on which the proceedings for possession are begun; and

(b) except where subsection (1)(b) of section 8 of this Act applies, was in arrears at the date of the service of the notice under that section relating to those proceedings.

Ground 11

Whether or not any rent is in arrears on the date on which proceedings for possession are begun, the tenant has persistently delayed paying rent which has become lawfully due.

Ground 12

Any obligation of the tenancy (other than one related to the payment of rent) has been broken or not performed.

Ground 13

The condition of the dwelling-house or any of the common parts has deteriorated owing to acts of waste by, or the neglect or default of, the tenant or any other person residing in the dwelling-house and, in the case of an act of waste by, or the neglect or default of, a person lodging with the tenant or a sub-tenant of his, the tenant has not taken such steps as he ought reasonably to have taken for the removal of the lodger or sub-tenant.

For the purposes of this ground, "common parts" means any part of a building comprising the dwelling-house and any other premises which the tenant is entitled under the terms of the tenancy to use in common with the occupiers of other dwelling-houses in which the landlord has an estate or interest.

Ground 14

The tenant or any other person residing in the dwelling-house has been guilty of conduct which is a nuisance or annoyance to adjoining occupiers, or has been convicted of using the dwelling-house or allowing the dwelling-house to be used for immoral or illegal purposes.

Ground 15

The condition of any furniture provided for use under the tenancy has, in the opinion of the court, deteriorated owing to ill-treatment by the tenant or any other person residing in the dwelling-house and, in the case of ill-treatment by a person lodging with the tenant or by a sub-tenant of his, the tenant has not taken such steps as he ought reasonably to have taken for the removal of the lodger or sub-tenant.

Ground 16

The dwelling-house was let to the tenant in consequence of his employment by the landlord seeking possession or a previous landlord under the tenancy and the tenant has ceased to be in that employment.

PART III

SUITABLE ALTERNATIVE ACCOMMODATION

1. For the purposes of Ground 9 above, a certificate of the local housing authority for the district in which the dwelling-house in question is situated, certifying that the authority will provide suitable alternative accommodation for the tenant by a date specified in the certificate, shall be conclusive evidence that suitable alternative accommodation will be available for him by that date.

2. Where no such certificate as is mentioned in paragraph 1 above is produced to the court, accommodation shall be deemed to be suitable for the purposes of Ground 9 above if it consists of either—

(a) premises which are to be let as a separate dwelling such that they will then be let on an assured tenancy, other than—

(i) a tenancy in respect of which notice is given not later than the beginning of the tenancy that possession might be recovered on any of Grounds 1 to 5 above, or

(ii) an assured shorthold tenancy, within the meaning of Chapter II of Part I of this Act, or

(b) premises to be let as a separate dwelling on terms which will, in the opinion of the court, afford to the tenant security of tenure reasonably equivalent to the security afforded by Chapter I of Part I of this Act in the case of an assured tenancy of a kind mentioned in sub-paragraph (a) above,

and, in the opinion of the court, the accommodation fulfils the relevant conditions as defined in paragraph 3 below.

3.—(1) For the purposes of paragraph 2 above, the relevant conditions are that the accommodation is reasonably suitable to the needs of the tenant and his family as regards proximity to place of work, and either—

(a) similar as regards rental and extent to the accommodation afforded by dwelling-houses provided in the neighbourhood by any local housing authority for persons whose needs as regards extent are, in the opinion of the court, similar to those of the tenant and of his family; or

(b) reasonably suitable to the means of the tenant and to the needs of the tenant and his family as regards extent and character; and

that if any furniture was provided for use under the assured tenancy in question, furniture is provided for use in the accommodation which is either similar to that so provided or is reasonably suitable to the needs of the tenant and his family.

(2) For the purposes of sub-paragraph (1)(a) above, a certificate of a local housing authority stating—

(a) the extent of the accommodation afforded by dwelling-houses provided by the authority to meet the needs of tenants with families of such number as may be specified in the certificate, and

(b) the amount of the rent charged by the authority for dwelling-houses affording accommodation of that extent,

shall be conclusive evidence of the facts so stated.

4. Accommodation shall not be deemed to be suitable to the needs of the tenant and his family if the result of their occupation of the accommodation would be that it would be an overcrowded dwelling-house for the purposes of Part X of the Housing Act 1985.

5. Any document purporting to be a certificate of a local housing authority named therein issued for the purposes of this Part of this Schedule and to be signed by the proper officer of that authority shall be received in evidence and, unless the contrary is shown, shall be deemed to be such a certificate without further proof.

6. In this Part of this Schedule "local housing authority" and "district", in relation to such an authority, have the same meaning as in the Housing Act 1985.

Part IV

Notices Relating to Recovery of Possession

7. Any reference in Grounds 1 to 5 in Part I of this Schedule or in the following provisions of this Part to the landlord giving a notice in writing to the tenant is, in the case of joint landlords, a reference to at least one of the joint landlords giving such a notice.

8.—(1) If, not later than the beginning of a tenancy (in this paragraph referred to as "the earlier tenancy"), the landlord gives such a notice in writing to the tenant as is mentioned in any of Grounds 1 to 5 in Part I of this Schedule, then, for the purposes of the ground in question and any further application of this paragraph, that notice shall also have effect as if it had been given immediately before the beginning of any later tenancy falling within sub-paragraph (2) below.

(2) Subject to sub-paragraph (3) below, sub-paragraph (1) above applies to a later tenancy—

    (a) which takes effect immediately on the coming to an end of the earlier tenancy; and

    (b) which is granted (or deemed to be granted) to the person who was the tenant under the earlier tenancy immediately before it came to an end; and

    (c) which is of substantially the same dwelling-house as the earlier tenancy.

(3) Sub-paragraph (1) above does not apply in relation to a later tenancy if, not later than the beginning of the tenancy, the landlord gave notice in writing to the tenant that the tenancy is not one in respect of which possession can be recovered on the ground in question.

9. Where paragraph 8(1) above has effect in relation to a notice given as mentioned in Ground 1 in Part I of this Schedule, the reference in paragraph (b) of that ground to the reversion on the tenancy is a reference to the reversion on the earlier tenancy and on any later tenancy falling within paragraph 8(2) above.

10. Where paragraph 8(1) above has effect in relation to a notice given as mentioned in Ground 3 or Ground 4 in Part I of this Schedule, any second or subsequent tenancy in relation to which the notice has effect shall be treated for the purpose of that ground as beginning at the beginning of the tenancy in respect of which the notice was actually given.

11. Any reference in Grounds 1 to 5 in Part I of this Schedule to a notice being given not later than the beginning of the tenancy is a reference to its being given not later than the day on which the tenancy is entered into and, accordingly, section 45(2) of this Act shall not apply to any such reference.

SCHEDULE 4

Statutory Tenants: Succession

Part I

Amendments of Schedule 1 to Rent Act 1977

1. In paragraph 1 the words "or, as the case may be, paragraph 3" shall be omitted.

2. At the end of paragraph 2 there shall be inserted the following sub-paragraphs—
    "(2) For the purposes of this paragraph, a person who was living with the

original tenant as his or her wife or husband shall be treated as the spouse of the original tenant.

(3) If, immediately after the death of the original tenant, there is, by virtue of sub-paragraph (2) above, more than one person who fulfils the conditions in sub-paragraph (1) above, such one of them as may be decided by agreement or, in default of agreement, by the county court shall be treated as the surviving spouse for the purposes of this paragraph."

3. In paragraph 3—

(a) after the words "residing with him" there shall be inserted "in the dwelling-house";

(b) for the words "period of 6 months" there shall be substituted "period of 2 years";

(c) for the words from "the statutory tenant" onwards there shall be substituted "entitled to an assured tenancy of the dwelling-house by succession"; and

(d) at the end there shall be added the following sub-paragraph—

"(2) If the original tenant died within the period of 18 months beginning on the operative date, then, for the purposes of this paragraph, a person who was residing in the dwelling-house with the original tenant at the time of his death and for the period which began 6 months before the operative date and ended at the time of his death shall be taken to have been residing with the original tenant for the period of 2 years immediately before his death."

4. In paragraph 4 the words "or 3" shall be omitted.

5. In paragraph 5—

(a) for the words from "or, as the case may be" to "of this Act" there shall be substituted "below shall have effect"; and

(b) for the words "the statutory tenant" there shall be substituted "entitled to an assured tenancy of the dwelling-house by succession".

6. For paragraph 6 there shall be substituted the following paragraph—

"6.—(1) Where a person who—

(a) was a member of the original tenant's family immediately before that tenant's death, and

(b) was a member of the first successor's family immediately before the first successor's death,

was residing in the dwelling-house with the first successor at the time of, and for the period of 2 years immediately before, the first successor's death, that person or, if there is more than one such person, such one of them as may be decided by agreement or, in default of agreement, by the county court shall be entitled to an assured tenancy of the dwelling-house by succession.

(2) If the first successor died within the period of 18 months beginning on the operative date, then, for the purposes of this paragraph, a person who was residing in the dwelling-house with the first successor at the time of his death and for the period which began 6 months before the operative date and ended at the time of his death shall be taken to have been residing with the first successor for the period of 2 years immediately before his death."

7. Paragraph 7 shall be omitted.

8. In paragraph 10(1)(a) for the words "paragraphs 6 or 7" there shall be substituted "paragraph 6".

9. At the end of paragraph 11 there shall be inserted the following paragraph—

> "11A. In this Part of this Schedule "the operative date" means the date on which Part I of the Housing Act 1988 came into force."

Part II

Amendments of Section 4 of Rent (Agriculture) Act 1976

10. In subsection (2) the words "or, as the case may be, subsection (4)" shall be omitted.

11. In subsection (4)—

(a) in paragraph (b) after the words "residing with him" there shall be inserted "in the dwelling-house" and for the words "period of six months" there shall be substituted "period of 2 years"; and

(b) for the words from "the statutory tenant" onwards there shall be substituted "entitled to an assured tenancy of the dwelling-house by succession".

12. In subsection (5) for the words "subsections (1), (3) and (4)" there shall be substituted "subsections (1) and (3)" and after that subsection there shall be inserted the following subsections—

> "(5A) For the purposes of subsection (3) above, a person who was living with the original occupier as his or her wife or husband shall be treated as the spouse of the original occupier and, subject to subsection (5B) below, the references in subsection (3) above to a widow and in subsection (4) above to a surviving spouse shall be construed accordingly.

> (5B) If, immediately after the death of the original occupier, there is, by virtue of subsection (5A) above, more than one person who fulfils the conditions in subsection (3) above, such one of them as may be decided by agreement or, in default of agreement by the county court, shall be the statutory tenant by virtue of that subsection.

> (5C) If the original occupier died within the period of 18 months beginning on the operative date, then, for the purposes of subsection (3) above, a person who was residing in the dwelling-house with the original occupier at the time of his death and for the period which began 6 months before the operative date and ended at the time of his death shall be taken to have been residing with the original occupier for the period of 2 years immediately before his death; and in this subsection "the operative date" means the date on which Part I of the Housing Act 1988 came into force."

Part III

Modifications of Section 7 and Schedule 2

13.—(1) Subject to sub-paragraph (2) below, in relation to the assured tenancy to which the successor becomes entitled by succession, section 7 of this Act shall have effect as if in subsection (3) after the word "established" there were inserted the words "or that the circumstances are as specified in any of Cases 11, 12, 16, 17, 18 and 20 in Schedule 15 to the Rent Act 1977".

(2) Sub-paragraph (1) above does not apply if, by virtue of section 39(8) of this Act, the assured tenancy to which the successor becomes entitled is an assured agricultural occupancy.

14. If by virtue of section 39(8) of this Act, the assured tenancy to which the successor becomes entitled is an assured agricultural occupancy, section 7 of this Act shall have effect in relation to that tenancy as if in subsection (3) after the word "established" there were inserted the words "or that the circumstances are as specified in Case XI or Case XII of the Rent (Agriculture) Act 1976".

15.—(1) In relation to the assured tenancy to which the successor becomes entitled by succession, any notice given to the predecessor for the purposes of Case 13, Case 14 or Case 15 in Schedule 15 to the Rent Act 1977 shall be treated as having been given for the purposes of whichever of Grounds 3 to 5 in Schedule 2 to this Act corresponds to the Case in question.

(2) Where sub-paragraph (1) above applies, the regulated tenancy of the predecessor shall be treated, in relation to the assured tenancy of the successor, as "the earlier tenancy" for the purposes of Part IV of Schedule 2 to this Act.

SCHEDULE 13

Amendments of Landlord and Tenant Act 1987

1. In Part I of the Landlord and Tenant Act 1987 (tenants' rights of first refusal), in section 2 (landlords for the purposes of Part I), in subsection (1) after "(2)" there shall be inserted "and section 4(1A)".

2.—(1) In section 3 of that Act (qualifying tenants), in subsection (1) (paragraphs (a) to (c) of which exclude certain tenants) the word "or" immediately preceding paragraph (c) shall be omitted and at the end of that paragraph there shall be added "or

(d) an assured tenancy or assured agricultural occupancy within the meaning of Part I of the Housing Act 1988".

(2) In subsection (2) of that section (which excludes persons having interests going beyond a particular flat), for paragraphs (a) and (b) there shall be substituted the words "by virtue of one or more tenancies none of which falls within paragraphs (a) to (d) of subsection (1), he is the tenant not only of the flat in question but also of at least two other flats contained in those premises"; and in subsection (3) of that section for "(2)(b)" there shall be substituted "(2)".

3.—(1) In section 4 of that Act (relevant disposals) after subsection (1) there shall be inserted the following subsection—

"(1A) Where an estate or interest of the landlord has been mortgaged, the reference in subsection (1) above to the disposal of an estate or interest by the landlord includes a reference to its disposal by the mortgagee in exercise of a power of sale or leasing, whether or not the disposal is made in the name of the landlord; and, in relation to such a proposed disposal by the mortgagee, any reference in the following provisions of this Part to the landlord shall be construed as a reference to the mortgagee."

(2) In subsection (2) of that section, in paragraph (a), at the end of sub-paragraph (i) there shall be inserted "or", sub-paragraph (ii) shall be omitted and at the end of that paragraph there shall be inserted—

"(aa) a disposal consisting of the creation of an estate or interest by way of security for a loan".

4.—(1) In Part III of that Act (compulsory acquisition by tenants of their landlord's interest), in section 26 (qualifying tenants), in subsection (2) (which excludes persons having interests going beyond a particular flat) for the words following "if" there shall be substituted "by virtue of one or more long leases none of which constitutes a tenancy to which Part II of the Landlord and Tenant Act 1954 applies, he is the tenant not only of the flat in question but also of at least two other flats contained in those premises".

(2) At the end of the said section 26 there shall be added the following subsection—

"(4) For the purposes of subsection (2) any tenant of a flat contained in the premises in question who is a body corporate shall be treated as the tenant of any other flat so contained and let to an associated company, as defined in section 20(1)."

5. In Part IV of that Act (variation of leases), for subsections (6) and (7) of section 35 (which make provision about long leases) there shall be substituted the following subsection—

"(6) For the purposes of this Part a long lease shall not be regarded as a long lease of a flat if—

(a) the demised premises consist of or include three or more flats contained in the same building; or

(b) the lease constitutes a tenancy to which Part II of the Landlord and Tenant Act 1954 applies."

6. In section 40 (application for variation of insurance provisions of lease of dwelling other than a flat) for subsection (4) (which makes provision about long leases) there shall be substituted the following subsections—

"(4) For the purpose of this section, a long lease shall not be regarded as a long lease of a dwelling if—

(a) the demised premises consist of three or more dwellings; or

(b) the lease constitutes a tenancy to which Part II of the Landlord and Tenant Act 1954 applies.

(4A) Without prejudice to subsection (4), an application under subsection (1) may not be made by a person who is a tenant under a long lease of a dwelling if, by virtue of that lease and one or more other long leases of dwellings, he is also a tenant from the same landlord of at least two other dwellings.

(4B) For the purposes of subsection (4A), any tenant of a dwelling who is a body corporate shall be treated as a tenant of any other dwelling held from the same landlord which is let under a long lease to an associated company, as defined in section 20(1)."

7. In Part VII of that Act (general), in section 58 (exempt landlords), in subsection (1) after paragraph (c) there shall be inserted the following paragraph—

"(ca) a housing action trust established under Part III of the Housing Act 1988."

SCHEDULE 14

APPOINTMENT ETC. OF RENT OFFICERS

PART I

AMENDMENTS OF SECTION 63 OF RENT ACT 1977

1. In subsection (1), paragraph (b) and the word "and" immediately preceding it shall be omitted.

2. In subsection (2)—

    (a) in paragraph (a) the words "and deputy rent officers" shall be omitted;

    (b) in paragraph (b) the words "or deputy rent officer" shall be omitted;

    (c) in paragraph (d) the words "and deputy rent officers" and the word "and" at the end of the paragraph shall be omitted; and

    (d) paragraph (e) shall be omitted.

3. After subsection (2) there shall be inserted the following subsection—

"(2A) A scheme under this section may make all or any of the following provisions—

    (a) provision requiring the consent of the Secretary of State to the appointment of rent officers;

    (b) provision with respect to the appointment of rent officers for fixed periods;

    (c) provision for the proper officer of the local authority, in such circumstances and subject to such conditions (as to consent or otherwise) as may be specified in the scheme,—

        (i) to designate a person appointed or to be appointed a rent officer as chief rent officer and to designate one or more such persons as senior rent officers;

        (ii) to delegate to a person so designated as chief rent officer such functions as may be specified in the scheme; and

        (iii) to revoke a designation under sub-paragraph (i) above and to revoke or vary a delegation under sub-paragraph (ii) above;

    (d) provision with respect to the delegation of functions by a chief rent officer to other rent officers (whether designated as senior rent officers or not);

    (e) provision as to the circumstances in which and the terms on which a rent officer appointed by the scheme may undertake functions outside the area to which the scheme relates in accordance with paragraph (f) below;

    (f) provision under which a rent officer appointed for an area other than that to which the scheme relates may undertake functions in the area to which the scheme relates and for such a rent officer to be treated for such purposes as may be specified in the scheme (which may include the purposes of paragraphs (c) and (d) above and paragraphs (c) and (d) of subsection (2) above) as if he were a rent officer appointed under the scheme; and

    (g) provision conferring functions on the proper officer of a local authority with respect to the matters referred to in paragraphs (d) to (f) above."

4. In subsection (3) the words "and deputy rent officers" shall be omitted.

5. In subsection (7)—

    (a) in paragraph (b) the words "and deputy rent officers" shall be omitted, after the words "section 7" there shall be inserted "or section 24" and for the words following "1972" there shall be substituted "or"; and

    (b) at the end of paragraph (b) there shall be inserted the following paragraph—

        "(c) incurred in respect of increases of pensions payable to or in respect of rent officers (so appointed) by virtue of the Pensions (Increase) Act 1971".

PART II

SECTIONS TO BE INSERTED IN RENT ACT 1977 AFTER SECTION 64

"Amalgamation schemes

64A.—(1) If the Secretary of State is of the opinion—

    (a) that there is at any time insufficient work in two or more registration areas to justify the existence of a separate service of rent officers for each area, or

    (b) that it would at any time be beneficial for the efficient administration of the service provided by rent officers in two or more registration areas,

he may, after consultation with the local authorities concerned, make a scheme under section 63 above designating as an amalgamated registration area the areas of those authorities and making provision accordingly for that amalgamated area.

(2) Any reference in the following provisions of this Chapter to a registration area includes a reference to an amalgamated registration area and, in relation to such an area, "the constituent authorities" means the local authorities whose areas make up the amalgamated area.

(3) A scheme under section 63 above made for an amalgamated registration area—

    (a) shall confer on the proper officer of one of the constituent authorities all or any of the functions which, in accordance with section 63 above, fall to be exercisable by the proper officer of the local authority for the registration area;

    (b) may provide that any rent officer previously appointed for the area of any one of the constituent authorities shall be treated for such purposes as may be specified in the scheme as a rent officer appointed for the amalgamated registration area; and

    (c) shall make such provision as appears to the Secretary of State to be appropriate for the payment by one or more of the constituent authorities of the remunerations, allowances and other expenditure which under section 63 above is to be paid by the local authority for the area.

(4) A scheme under section 63 above made for an amalgamated registration area may contain such incidental, transitional and supplementary provisions as appear to the Secretary of State to be necessry or expedient.

New basis for administration of rent officer service

64B.—(1) If, with respect to registration areas generally or any particular registration area or areas, it appears to the Secretary of State that it is no longer appropriate for the appointment, remuneration and administration of rent officers to be a function of local authorities, he may by order—

(a) provide that no scheme under section 63 above shall be made for the area or areas specified in the order; and

(b) make, with respect to the area or areas so specified, such provision as appears to him to be appropriate with respect to the appointment, remuneration and administration of rent officers and the payment of pensions, allowances or gratuities to or in respect of them.

(2) An order under this section shall make provision for any expenditure attributable to the provisions of the order to be met by the Secretary of State in such manner as may be specified in the order (whether by way of grant, reimbursement or otherwise); and any expenditure incurred by the Secretary of State by virtue of this subsection shall be paid out of money provided by Parliament.

(3) An order under this section—

(a) may contain such incidental, transitional and supplementary provisions as appear to the Secretary of State to be appropriate, including provisions amending this Part of this Act; and

(b) shall be made by statutory instrument which shall be subject to annulment in pursuance of a resolution of either House of Parliament."

Relevant Statutory Instruments and Prescribed Forms

STATUTORY INSTRUMENTS

1982 No. 1474

LANDLORD AND TENANT

The Rent Book (Forms of Notice) Regulations 1982

Made	15th October 1982
Laid before Parliament	27th October 1982
Coming into Operation	1st January 1983

The Secretary of State for the Environment, as respects England, and the Secretary of State for Wales, as respects Wales, in exercise of powers conferred by section 2(1) and 6(1)(*b*) of the Landlord and Tenant Act 1962(a) and now vested in them(b) and of all other powers enabling them in that behalf, hereby make the following regulations:—

1. These regulations may be cited as the Rent Book (Forms of Notice) Regulations 1982 and shall come into operation on 1st January 1983.

2. In these regulations:—

"the 1962 Act" means the Landlord and Tenant Act 1962;
"the 1976 Act" means the Rent (Agriculture) Act 1976(c); and
"the 1977 Act" means the Rent Act 1977(d).

3.—(1) The prescribed form in which, under section 2(1) of the 1962 Act, notice or particulars are required to be contained in a rent book or other similar document provided in pursuance of section 1 of the 1962 Act shall be as follows.—

(*a*) if the premises are occupied by virtue of a restricted contract within the meaning of the 1977 Act, the form set out in Part I of the Schedule to these regulations;

(*b*) if the premises are a dwelling house let on or subject to a protected or statutory

---

(a) 1962 c.50; section 2(1) was amended by the Rent Act 1968 (c.23), Schedule 15, by the Rent (Agriculture) Act 1976 (c.80), Schedule 8, paragraph 9 and the Rent Act 1977 (c.42), Schedule 23, paragraph 31
(b) S.I. 1970/1681   (c) 1976 c.80.   (d) 1977 c.42.

tenancy within the meaning of the 1977 Act, the form set out in Part II of the Schedule to these regulations; and

(c) if the premises are a dwelling house subject to a statutory tenancy as defined in the 1976 Act, the form set out in Part III of the Schedule to these regulations

or, in each case, a form substantially to the same effect.

(2) In the cases referred to in paragraphs (a), (b) and (c) above, such rent book or similar document shall contain notice of the matters set out in the appropriate prescribed form, in addition to the name and address of the landlord and the particulars required by section 2(1) of the 1962 Act.

4. The Rent Book (Forms of Notice) Regulations 1976(a) are hereby revoked.

SCHEDULE

Part I

(Form for Rent Book for Restricted Contract)

INFORMATION FOR TENANT

IMPORTANT—PLEASE READ THIS
If the rent for the premises you occupy as your residence is payable weekly, the landlord must provide you with a rent book or similar document. If you have a "restricted contract" (see paragraph 9 below), the rent book or similar document must contain this notice, properly filled in.

---

1.   Address of premises ....

....

*2.   Name and address of landlord ....

....

*3.   Name and address of agent (if any) ....

....

*4.   The rent payable including/excluding† rates is £ .... per week.

If a reasonable rent is registered by the Rent Tribunal, paragraph 5 and, where it applies, paragraph 6 must be filled in, otherwise they should be crossed out.

---

*5.   The registered rent (which excludes rates) is £ .... per week,

registered on .... (date).

*6.   In addition to the registered rent, £ .... per week is payable to cover rates paid by the landlord or a superior landlord.

(a) S.I. 1976/378.
* These entries must be kept up-to-date.
† Cross out whichever does not apply.

7. Details of accommodation (if any) which the occupier has the right to share with other persons ....

....

....

8. The other terms and conditions of the contract are ....

....

....

9. *Restricted contracts* are usually lettings by landlords who live in the same house. There are rules about your rights to stay in the accommodation and the rent you pay for restricted contracts. Full details are given in the Department of the Environment and Welsh Office booklets "Letting Rooms in Your Home" and "Notice to Quit", nos. 4 and 11 in the series of housing booklets. These booklets are obtainable free from rent officers, council offices and housing aid centres, some of which also give advice.

10. If your letting began on or after 28th November 1980, you cannot be evicted unless the landlord gets a possession order from the courts. The rules for lettings which began before 28th November 1980 are different. You may have the right to apply to the Rent Tribunal to postpone any notice to quit and the landlord often also needs a court order. Whether your letting began before or after 28th November 1980, either you or the landlord can apply to the Rent Tribunal to fix a reasonable rent. It is unwise to apply without first getting advice.

11. You may be entitled to get help to pay your rent. Apply to your local council for details of the rent allowance and rate rebate schemes.

12. It is a criminal offence for your landlord to harass you or interfere with your possessions or use of facilities in order to force you to leave.

13. If you are in any doubt about your legal rights or obligations, particularly if your landlord has asked you to leave, you should go to a Citizens' Advice Bureau, housing aid centre, law centre or solicitor. Help with all or part of the cost of legal advice from a solicitor may be available under the Legal Aid Scheme.

PART II

(FORM FOR RENT BOOK FOR PROTECTED OR STATUTORY TENANCY)

INFORMATION FOR TENANT

> **IMPORTANT—PLEASE READ THIS**
> If the rent for the premises you occupy as your residence is payable weekly, the landlord must provide you with a rent book or similar document. If you have a protected or statutory tenancy (see paragraph 9 below), the rent book or similar document must contain this notice, properly filled in.

1. Address of premises ....

....

*2. Name and address of landlord ....

....

*3. Name and address of agent (if any) ....

....

*4. The rent payable including/excluding† rates is £ .... per week.

> *If a fair rent is registered paragraph 5 and, where it applies, paragraph 6 must be filled in, otherwise they should be crossed out.*

*5. The registered rent (which excludes rates) is £ .... per week.

effective from .... (date).
If the rent is registered as variable (because it includes service charges which vary), this should be indicated by placing a tick in the box□.

*6. In addition to the registered rent, £ .... per week is payable to cover rates paid by the landlord or superior landlord.

7. Details of the accommodation (if any) which the occupier has the right to share with other persons ....

....

....

8. The other terms and conditions of the tenancy are ....

....

....

9. You are protected by the Rent Act 1977 and known as a "regulated tenant". The Rent Act contains important rules concerning the amount of rent you have to pay and your rights to stay in your home. Details of these rules are set out in the Department of the Environment and Welsh Office booklets "Regulated Tenancies" and "Notice to Quit", nos. 7 and 11 in the series of housing booklets. These booklets are available from rent officers, council offices and housing aid centres, some of which also give advice.

10. Either you or your landlord may apply to the rent officer for a fair rent to be registered. It is wise to get advice before doing so. Whether or not your rent is registered by the rent officer there are rules about how and when it can be increased. You cannot be evicted from your home unless your landlord gets a possession order from the courts, and the courts can grant an order only in special circumstances.

11. If you have a protected *shorthold* tenancy, special rules apply. You should read housing booklet no. 8 "Shorthold Tenancies—First Revision" which sets out these rules.

12. The Housing Act 1980 converted most *controlled* tenancies into regulated tenancies. If your tenancy was formerly a controlled one, you should read housing booklet no. 6 "Controlled Tenancies" which explains your position.

---

*These entries must be kept up-to-date.
† Cross out whichever does not apply.

13. You may be entitled to get help to pay your rent. Apply to your local council for details of the rent allowance and rate rebate schemes.

14. It is a criminal offence for your landlord to evict you without an order from the court or to harass you or interfere with your possessions or use of facilities in order to force you to leave.

15. If you are in any doubt about your legal rights or obligations, particularly if your landlord has asked you to leave, you should go to a Citizens Advice Bureau, housing aid centre, law centre or solicitor. Help with all or part of the cost of legal advice from a solicitor may be available under the Legal Aid Scheme.

PART III

(FORM FOR RENT BOOK FOR TENANCY UNDER THE RENT
(AGRICULTURE) ACT 1976)

INFORMATION FOR TENANT

> IMPORTANT—PLEASE READ THIS
> If the rent for the premises you occupy as your residence is payable weekly, the landlord must provide you with a rent book or similar document. If you have a statutory tenancy under the Rent (Agriculture) Act 1976 (see paragraph 9 below), the rent book or similar document must contain this notice, properly filled in.

*1. Address of premises ....

....

*2. Name and address of landlord ....

....

*3. Name and address of agent (if any) ....

....

*4. The rent payable (or to be deducted from pay) including/excluding† rates is £ .... per week.

> *If a fair rent is registered paragraph 5 and, where it applies, paragraph 6 must be filled in, otherwise they should be crossed out.*

*5. The registered rent (which excludes rates) is £ ....
per week, effective from .... (date).
If the rent is registered as variable (because it includes service charges which vary), this should be indicated by placing a tick in the box □.

*6. In addition to the registered rent, £ ...... per week is payable to cover rates paid by the landlord or superior landlord.

7. Details of accommodation (if any) which the occupier has the right to share with other

---

* These entries must be kept up-to-date.
† Cross out whichever does not apply.

persons ....

....

....

8. The other terms and conditions of the tenancy are ....

....

....

9. You are protected by the Rent (Agriculture) Act 1976, and known as a "statutory tenant" under that Act. The Act contains important rules concerning the amount of rent you have to pay and your rights to stay in your home. Details of these rules are set out in the booklet "Some Questions and Answers about the Rent (Agriculture) Act 1976". This booklet is available free from rent officers, council offices and housing aid centres, some of which also give advice.

10. The rules about the amount of rent you can be charged depend on whether a fair rent has been registered by the rent officer. If a fair rent has been registered, that is the most that your landlord can charge. If no fair rent is registered, the landlord can charge a provisional rent at a yearly level currently fixed at $1\frac{1}{2}$ times the rateable value of your cottage. There is nothing to prevent you and your landlord agreeing upon a lower figure. You cannot be evicted from your home unless your landlord gets a possession order from the courts. The courts can grant an order only if suitable alternative accommodation is made available to you or in certain other special cases.

11. You may be entitled to get help to pay your rent. Apply to your local council for details of the rent allowance and rate rebate schemes.

12. It is a criminal offence for your landlord to evict you without an order from the court or to harass you or interfere with your possessions or use of facilities in order to force you to leave.

13. If you are in doubt about your legal rights or obligations, particularly if your landlord has asked you to leave, you should go to a Citizens Advice Bureau, housing aid centre, law centre or solicitor. Help with all or part of the cost of legal advice from a solicitor may be available under the Legal Aid Scheme.

EXPLANATORY NOTE

(This Note is not part of the Regulations)

Under the provisions of section 1 of the Landlord and Tenant Act 1962, where a person has the right to occupy any premises as a residence in consideration of a rent which is payable weekly, it is the duty of the landlord to provide a rent book or other similar document for use in respect of the premises.

These regulations, which supersede the Rent Book (Forms of Notice) Regulations 1976, revise the notices which, under the 1962 Act, are to be contained in rent books or other similar documents provided in pursuance of that Act, in the case of:—

(1) premises occupied by virtue of a restricted contract under the Rent Act 1977;

(2) premises let on or subject to a protected or statutory tenancy under the Rent Act 1977; and

(3) premises subject to a statutory tenancy as defined in the Rent (Agriculture) Act 1976.

These notices are revised to provide a form of notice of case (3) above (the Rent (Agriculture) Act 1976 was passed after the 1976 Regulations were made) and to take account in particular of changes in the Rent Act 1977 effected by Part II of the Housing Act 1980 (c.51).

STATUTORY INSTRUMENTS

1988 No. 2198

LANDLORD AND TENANT, ENGLAND AND WALES

The Rent Book (Forms of Notice) (Amendment) Regulations 1988

Made	14th December 1988
Laid before Parliament	22nd December 1988
Coming into force	15th January 1989

The Secretary of State for the Environment, as respects England, and the Secretary of State for Wales, as respects Wales, in exercise of the powers conferred on them by section 5 of the Landlord and Tenant Act 1985(**a**), and of all other powers enabling them in that behalf, hereby make the following Regulations:

1. These Regulations may be cited as the Rent Book (Forms of Notice) (Amendment) Regulations 1988 and shall come into force on 15th January 1989.

2. The Rent Book (Forms of Notice) Regulations 1982(**b**) are amended as follows–

(1) at the end of regulation 2 insert–
"and
"the 1988 Act" means the Housing Act 1988";

(2) after regulation 3(1)(c) insert–
"(d) if the premises are a dwelling house let on an assured tenancy or an assured agricultural occupancy within the meaning of the 1988 Act, the form set out in Part IV of the Schedule to these regulations";

(3) in regulation 3(2) for "(a), (b) and (c)" substitute "(a) to (d)";

(4) substitute for the words in paragraph 11 of the forms in Parts I and III of the Schedule and in paragraph 13 of the form in Part II of the Schedule "You may be entitled to get help to pay your rent and rates through the housing benefit scheme. Apply to your local council for details.";

(5) for paragraphs 11 and 12 of the form in Part II of the Schedule substitute "11. If you have a protected shorthold tenancy or your tenancy was formerly a controlled one, special rules apply."; and

(6) insert as Part IV of the Schedule the form in the Schedule to these Regulations.

(**a**) 1985 c.70; section 5 was amended by paragraph 67 of Schedule 17 to the Housing Act 1988 (c.50).
(**b**) S.I. 1982/1474.

SCHEDULE

(FORM FOR RENT BOOK FOR ASSURED TENANCY OR ASSURED AGRICULTURAL OCCUPANCY)

IMPORTANT—PLEASE READ THIS

If the rent for the premises you occupy as your residence is payable weekly, the landlord must provide you with a rent book or similar document. If you have an assured tenancy, including an assured *shorthold* tenancy (*see* paragraph 7 below), or an assured agricultural occupancy, the rent book or similar document must contain this notice, properly filled in.

---

1.   Address of premises ....

     ....

*2.   Name and address of landlord ....

     ....

*3.   Name and address of agent (if any) ....

     ....

*4.   The rent payable including/excluding† rates is £ .... per week.

5.   Details of accommodation (if any) which the occupier has the right to share with other persons ....

6.   The other terms and conditions of the tenancy are ....

     ....

     ....

     ....

     ....

7.   If you have an assured tenancy or an assured agricultural occupancy you have certain rights under the Housing Act 1988. These include the right not to be evicted from your home unless your landlord gets a possession order from the courts. Unless the property is let under an assured *shorthold* tenancy, the courts can only grant an order on a limited number of grounds. Further details regarding assured tenancies are set out in the Department of the Environment and Welsh Office booklet "Assured Tenancies" no. 19 in the series of housing booklets. These booklets are available from rent officers, council offices and housing aid centres, some of which also give advice.

8.   You may be entitled to get help to pay your rent and rates through the housing benefit scheme. Apply to your local council for details.

9.   It is a criminal offence for your landlord to evict you without an order from the court or to harass you or interfere with your possessions or use of facilities in order to force you to leave.

---

* These entries must be kept up-to-date.
† Cross out whichever does not apply.

10.   If you are in any doubt about your legal rights or obligations, particularly if your landlord has asked you to leave, you should go to a Citizens' Advice Bureau, housing aid centre, law centre or solicitor. Help with all or part of the cost of legal advice from a solicitor may be available under the Legal Aid Scheme.

EXPLANATORY NOTE

(This note is not part of the Regulations)

These Regulations amend the Rent Book (Forms of Notice) Regulations 1982 by adding a form of notice which (under section 5 of the Landlord and Tenant Act 1985 as amended by the Housing Act 1988) is to be inserted in rent books or other similar documents. The new form of notice relates to premises let on or subject to an assured tenancy or an assured agricultural occupancy.

STATUTORY INSTRUMENTS

1988 No. 2201

LANDLORD AND TENANT, ENGLAND AND WALES

The Notices to Quit etc. (Prescribed Information) Regulations 1988

Made	14th December 1988
Laid before Parliament	22nd December 1988
Coming into force	15th January 1989

The Secretary of State for the Environment, as respects England, and the Secretary of State for Wales, as respects Wales, in exercise of the powers conferred upon them by section 5 of the Protection from Eviction Act 1977(a), and of all other powers enabling them in that behalf, hereby make the following Regulations:

1.   These Regulations may be cited as the Notices to Quit etc. (Prescribed Information) Regulations 1988 and shall come into force on 15th January 1989.

2.   Where, on or after the date these Regulations come into force, a landlord gives a notice to quit any premises let as a dwelling, or a licensor gives a notice to determine a periodic licence to occupy premises as a dwelling (and the premises are not let or occupied as specified in section 5(1B) of the Protection from Eviction Act 1977), the information prescribed for the purposes of section 5 of the Protection from Eviction Act 1977 shall be that in the Schedule to these Regulations.

3.   The Notices to Quit (Prescribed Information) Regulations 1980(b) are hereby revoked.

SCHEDULE

PRESCRIBED INFORMATION

1.   If the tenant or licensee does not leave the dwelling, the landlord or licensor must get an order for possession from the court before the tenant or licensee can lawfully be evicted. The landlord or licensor cannot apply for such an order before the notice to quit or notice to determine has run out.

2.   A tenant or licensee who does not know if he has any right to remain in possession after a notice to quit or a notice to determine runs out can obtain advice from a solicitor. Help with all or part of the cost of legal advice and assistance may be available under the Legal Aid Scheme. He should also be able to obtain information from a Citizens' Advice Bureau, a Housing Aid Centre or a rent officer.

(a) 1977 c.43; section 5 was amended by the Housing Act 1988 (c.50), section 32.   (b) S.I. 1980/1624.

EXPLANATORY NOTE

(This note is not part of the Regulations)

These Regulations prescribe the information to be contained in a landlord's notice to quit given on or after the 15th January 1989 to determine a tenancy of premises let as a dwelling, or a licensor's notice given on or after that date to determine a periodic licence to occupy premises as a dwelling. They do not apply to the premises specified in section 5(1B) of the Protection from Eviction Act 1977 (premises subject to excluded licences or certain excluded tenancies). These Regulations replace the Notices to Quit (Prescribed Information) Regulations 1980, which applied only to tenancies.

STATUTORY INSTRUMENTS

1988 No. 2203

LANDLORD AND TENANT, ENGLAND AND WALES

The Assured Tenancies and Agricultural Occupancies (Forms) Regulations 1988

Made	14th December 1988
Coming into force	15th January 1989

The Secretary of State for the Environment, as respects England, and the Secretary of State for Wales, as respects Wales, in exercise of the powers conferred upon them by sections 6(2) and (3), 8(3), 13(2) and (4), 20(2), 22(1), 41(2) and 45(1) and (5) of the Housing Act 1988(a), and of all other powers enabling them in that behalf, hereby make the following Regulations:

1. These Regulations may be cited as the Assured Tenancies and Agricultural Occupancies (Forms) Regulations 1988 and shall come into force on 15th January 1989.

2. In these Regulations any reference to a section is to a section of the Housing Act 1988 and any reference to a numbered form is a reference to the form bearing that number in the Schedule to these Regulations, or to a form substantially to the same effect.

3. The forms prescribed for the purposes of Part I of the Housing Act 1988 shall be as follows–

(1) for a notice under section 6(2) proposing terms of a statutory periodic tenancy different from the implied terms, form no. 1;

(2) for an application under section 6(3) referring a notice under section 6(2) to a rent assessment committee, form no. 2;

(3) for a notice under section 8 informing a tenant that the landlord intends to begin proceedings for possession of a dwelling-house let on an assured tenancy which is not an assured agricultural occupancy, form no. 3;

(4) for a notice under section 8 informing a tenant that the landlord intends to begin proceedings for possession of a dwelling-house let on an assured agricultural occupancy, form no. 4;

(5) for a notice under section 13(2) proposing a new rent for an assured tenancy or an assured agricultural occupancy, form no. 5;

(6) for an application under section 13(4) referring to a rent assessment committee a notice under section 13(2) relating to an assured tenancy or an assured agricultural occupancy, form no. 6;

(7) for a notice under section 20 of intention to grant an assured shorthold tenancy, form no. 7;

(8) for an application under section 22(1) to a rent assessment committee for a determination of rent under an assured shorthold tenancy, form no. 8; and

---

(a) 1988 c.50; in section 45(1), *see* the definition of "prescribed".

(9) for a notice under section 41(2) requiring a landlord or tenant to give information to a rent assessment committee, form no. 9.

SCHEDULE

FORM No. 1

Housing Act 1988 section 6(2)

Notice Proposing Different Terms for Statutory Periodic Tenancy

- Please write clearly in black ink.

- **This notice proposes changes to the terms of the statutory periodic tenancy. If you wish to refer it to a rent assessment committee you must keep to the time limit set out in paragraph 2 below.**

- Please read this notice very carefully as it may alter the terms of the statutory periodic tenancy which arises when a fixed term assured tenancy runs out. It may also be used when a fixed term assured agricultural occupancy ends.

- It can be used by either a landlord or a tenant.

- This notice must be served no later than the first anniversary of the day the former fixed term tenancy or occupancy ended.

- Do not use this notice if you are a landlord only proposing an increase in rent.

- If you need help or advice about this notice. and what you should do about it. take it immediately to any of the following:
  - a Citizens' Advice Bureau
  - a housing aid centre.
  - a law centre or a solicitor.

1. To: ⬚ *Name(s) of landlord(s) or tenant(s)**

   of: ⬚ *Address of premises*

2. This is to give notice that I/we* propose different terms of the statutory periodic tenancy from those in the fixed term assured tenancy which has now ended to take effect from

   ⬚ 19

This date must be at least three months after this notice is served.

*Cross out whichever does not apply.

- If you agree with the new terms and rent proposed. do nothing. They will become the terms of your tenancy agreement on the date specified in paragraph 2.
- If you don't agree with the proposed terms and any adjustment of the rent (see paragraph 4). and you are unable to reach agreement with your landlord/tenant. or you do not wish to discuss it with him, you may refer the matter directly to your local rent assessment committee. **within three months of the date on which the notice was served,** using a special form.
- The committee will determine the proposed changes in the terms of the tenancy or some other different terms covering the same points. and the appropriate level of rent. if this applies.

3. Changes to the terms

    (a)   The provisions of the tenancy to be changed are–
          Please attach relevant sections of the agreement if available.

    (b)   The proposed changes are–
          (Continue on a separate sheet if necessary.)

4.*Changes to the rent, if applicable

    The existing rent is
    This includes rates*

£	per

eg. week, month, year

    The new rent which takes into account
    the proposed changes in the terms of the tenancy
    will be–

£	per

eg. week, month, year

    This includes rates*

- Changes to the rent are optional. A proposal to adjust the rent to take account of the proposed new terms at paragraph 3 may be made if either the landlord or the tenant considers it appropriate.

To be signed by the landlord or his agent (someone acting for him) or the tenant or his agent. If there are joint landlords or joint tenants each landlord/tenant or the agent must sign unless one signs on behalf of the rest with their agreement.

Signed

*Name(s) of land-
lord(s)/tenant(s)*

*Address of land-
lord(s)/tenant(s)*

Tel:

If signed by agent, name and address of agent

Tel: *Date:*   19

Cross out if this does not apply.

FORM No. 2

Housing Act 1988 section 6(3)

Application Referring a Notice Under Section 6(2) to a Rent Assessment Committee

- Please write clearly in black ink.
- Please tick boxes where appropriate.
- When you have filled the form in please send it to the appropriate rent assessment panel.
- Make sure you also send a copy of the notice served on you proposing the new terms of the statutory periodic tenancy.

- This application may be used by a landlord or a tenant who has been served with a notice under section 6(2) of the Housing Act 1988. varying the terms of a statutory periodic tenancy. It may also be used where there was an earlier assured agricultural occupancy.

1. Address of premises

2. Name(s) of tenant(s)

3. Name(s) of landlord(s)

   Address of landlord(s)

4. Details of premises.

   (a) What type of property is it. eg house, flat or room(s)?

   (b) If it is a flat or room(s) say what floor(s) it is on.

   (c) Give the number and type of rooms, eg living room, bathroom.

   (d) Does the tenancy include any other facilities, eg garden, garage or other separate building or land?   Yes ☐   No ☐

   (e) If Yes, please give details.

   (f) Is any of the accommodation shared?
       (i) with the landlord?   Yes ☐   No ☐
       (ii) with another tenant or tenants?   Yes ☐   No ☐

   (g) If Yes, please give details.

5. What is the current rateable value of the premises?

£

6. When did the statutory tenancy begin?

19

7. Services

    (a) Are any services provided under the tenancy (eg cleaning, lighting, heating, hot water or gardening)?

        Yes ☐   No ☐

    (b) If Yes, please give details.

    (c) Is a separate charge made for services, maintenance, repairs, landlord's costs of management or any other item?

        Yes ☐   No ☐

    (d) What charge is payable?

£

    (e) Does the charge vary according to the relevant costs?

        Yes ☐   No ☐

    (f) If Yes, please give details.

8. (a) Is any furniture provided under the tenancy?

        Yes ☐   No ☐

    (b) If Yes, please give details
(*continue on a separate sheet if necessary*).

9. What repairs are the responsibility of
    (a) the landlord?

    (b) the tenant?
(*continue on a separate sheet if necessary*).

10. (a) Give details of the other terms of the tenancy, eg whether the tenancy is assignable and whether a premium may be charged on an assignment
(*continue on a separate sheet if necessary*).

    (b) Please attach the tenancy agreement (or a copy), with a note of any variations, if you have one. It will be returned to you without delay.

11. I/We* attach a copy of the notice proposing changes to the statutory periodic tenancy and, if applicable, an adjustment of the amount of rent and apply to the rent assessment committee to consider it.

Cross out whichever does not apply.

To be signed by the landlord or his agent (someone acting for him), or by the tenant or his agent. If there are joint landlords or joint tenants each landlord/tenant or the agent must sign, unless one signs on behalf of the rest with their agreement.

Signed

Name(s) of land-
lord(s)/tenant(s)

Address of land-
lord(s)/tenant(s)

Tel:

If signed by agent, name and address of agent

Tel: Date: 19

FORM No. 3

Housing Act 1988 section 8

Notice Seeking Possession of a Property
Let on an Assured Tenancy

- Please write clearly in black ink.

- Do not use this form if possession is sought from an assured shorthold tenant under section 21 of the Housing Act 1988 or if the property is occupied under an assured agricultural occupancy.

- **This notice is the first step towards requiring you to give up possession of your home. You should read it very carefully.**

- If you need advice about this notice, and what you should do about it, take it as quickly as possible to any of the following–

  - a Citizens' Advice Bureau.

  - a housing aid centre.

  - a law centre.

  - or a solicitor.

  You may be able to get Legal Aid but this will depend on your personal circumstances.

1. **To:** ▢   *Name(s) of tenant(s)*

2. **Your landlord intends to apply to the court for an order requiring you to give up possession of–**

   ▢   *Address of premises*

- If you have an assured tenancy under the Housing Act 1988, which is not an assured shorthold tenancy, you can only be required to leave your home if your landlord gets an order for possession from the court on one of the grounds which are set out in Schedule 2 to the Act.

- If you are willing to give up possession of your home without a court order, you should tell the person who signed this notice as soon as possible and say when you can leave.

3. **The landlord intends to seek possession on ground(s)** ▢ **in Schedule 2 to the Housing Act 1988, which reads**

   Give the full text of each ground which is being relied on. (Continue on a separate sheet if necessary.)

   ▢

- Whichever grounds are set out in paragraph 3 the court may allow any of the other grounds to be added at a later date. If this is done, you will be told about it so you can discuss the additional grounds at the court hearing as well as the grounds set out in paragraph 3.

4. **Particulars of each ground are as follows–**

   Give a full explanation of why each ground is being relied on. (Continue on a separate sheet if necessary.)

   ▢

- If the court is satisfied that any of grounds 1 to 8 is established it must make an order (but see below in respect of fixed term tenancies).

- Before the court will grant an order on any of grounds 9 to 16, it must be satisfied that it is reasonable to require you to leave. This means that, if one of these grounds is set out in paragraph 3, you will be able to suggest to the court that it is not reasonable that you should have to leave, even if you accept that the ground applies.

- The court will not make an order under grounds 1, 3 to 7, 9 or 16, to take effect during the fixed term of the tenancy: and it will only make an order during the fixed term on grounds 2, 8 or 10 to 15 if the terms of the tenancy make provision for it to be brought to an end on any of these grounds.

- Where the court makes an order for possession solely on ground 6 or 9, your landlord must pay your reasonable removal expenses.

5. The court proceedings will not begin until after

	19

Give the date after which court proceedings can be brought.

- Where the landlord is seeking possession under grounds 1, 2, 5 to 7, 9 or 16 in Schedule 2, court proceedings cannot begin earlier than 2 months from the date this notice is served on you and not before the date on which the tenancy (had it not been assured) could have been brought to an end by a notice to quit served at the same time as this notice.

- Where the landlord is seeking possession on grounds 3, 4, 8 or 10 to 15, court proceedings cannot begin until 2 weeks after the date this notice is served.

- After the date shown in paragraph 5, court proceedings may be begun at once but not later than 12 months from the date this notice is served. After this time the notice will lapse and a new notice must be served before possession can be sought.

To be signed by the landlord or his agent (someone acting for him).

Signed

Name(s) of landlord(s)

Address of landlord(s)

Tel:

If signed by agent, name and address of agent

Tel: *Date:*   19

FORM No. 4

Housing Act 1988 section 8

Notice Seeking Possession of an
Assured Agricultural Occupancy

- Please write clearly in black ink.
- This notice is the first step towards requiring you to give up possession of your home. You should read it very carefully.
- If you need advice about this notice, and what you should do about it, take it as quickly as possible to any of the following—

- a Citizens' Advice Bureau,
- a housing aid centre,
- a law centre,
- or a solicitor.

You may be able to get Legal Aid but this will depend on your personal circumstances.

1. To:

    Name(s) of tenant(s) or licensee(s)

2. Your landlord or licensor intends to apply to the court for an order requiring you to give up possession of—

    Address of premises

- If you have an assured agricultural occupancy under the Housing Act 1988, which is not an assured shorthold tenancy, you can only be required to leave your home if your landlord or licensor gets an order for possession from the court on one of the grounds which are set out in Schedule 2 to the Act, except ground 16.

- If you are willing to give up possession of your home without a court order, you should tell the person who signed this notice as soon as possible and say when you can leave.

3. The landlord or licensor intends to seek possession on ground(s) ⬚ in Schedule 2 to the Housing Act 1988, which reads

    Give the full text of each ground which is being relied on. Continue on a separate sheet if necessary.)

- Whichever grounds are set out in paragraph 3 the court may allow any of the other grounds to be added at a later date. If this is done, you will be told about it so you can discuss the additional grounds at the court hearing as well as the grounds set out in paragraph 3.

4. Particulars of each ground are as follows—

    Give a full explanation of why each ground is being relied on. (Continue on a separate sheet if necessary.)

- If the court is satisfied that any of grounds 1 to 8 is established it must make an order (but see below in respect of fixed term tenancies or licences).

- Before the court will grant an order on any of grounds 9 to 15, it must be satisfied that it is reasonable to require you to leave. This means that, if one of these grounds is set out in paragraph 3, you will be able to suggest to the court that it is not reasonable that you should have to leave, even if you accept that the ground applies.

- The court will not make an order under grounds 1, 3 to 7 or 9, to take effect during the fixed term of the tenancy or licence; and it will only make an order during the fixed term on grounds 2, 8 or 10 to 15 if the terms of the tenancy or licence make provision for it to be brought to an end on any of these grounds.

- Where the court makes an order for possession solely on ground 6 or 9, your landlord or licensor must pay your reasonable removal expenses.

5. The court proceedings will not begin until after

19

Give the date after which court proceedings can be brought.

- Where the landlord or licensor is seeking possession under grounds 1, 2, 5 to 7 or 9 in Schedule 2, court proceedings cannot begin earlier than 2 months from the date this notice is served on you and not before the date on which the tenancy or licence (had it not been an assured agricultural occupancy) could have been brought to an end by a notice to quit or determine served at the same time as this notice.

- Where the landlord or licensor is seeking possession on grounds 3, 4, 8 or 10 to 15, court proceedings cannot begin until 2 weeks after the date this notice is served.

- After the date shown in paragraph 5, court proceedings may be begun at once but not later than 12 months from the date this notice is served. After this time the notice will lapse and a new notice must be served before possession can be sought.

To be signed by the landlord, the licensor or his agent (someone acting for him).

Signed

Name(s) of
landlord(s)
or licensor(s)

Address of
landlord(s)
or licensor(s)

Tel:

If signed by agent, name and address of agent

Tel: Date: 19

FORM No. 5

Housing Act 1988 section 13(2)

Landlord's Notice Proposing a New Rent Under An Assured Periodic Tenancy or Agricultural Occupancy

- Please write clearly in black ink.

- Do not use this form if there is a current rent fixing mechanism in the tenancy.

- Do not use this form to propose a rent adjustment for a statutory periodic tenancy solely because of a proposed change of terms under section 6(2) of the Housing Act 1988.

- This notice may also be used to propose a new rent or licence fee for an assured agricultural occupancy. In such a case references to "landlord"/"tenant" can be read as references to "licensor"/"licensee" etc.

- **This notice proposes a new rent. If you want to oppose this proposal you must keep to the time limit set out in paragraph 2.** Read this notice carefully. If you need help or advice take it immediately to:
  - a Citizens' Advice Bureau.
  - a housing aid centre.
  - a law centre.
  - or a solicitor.

1. To: _____   *Name(s) of tenant(s)*

   of: _____   *Address of premises*

2. This is to give notice that as from _____ 19____

   your landlord proposes to charge a new rent.

   The new rent must take effect at the beginning of a new period of the tenancy and not earlier than any of the following–

   (a) the minimum period after this notice was served,
   (The minimum period is–
   - in the case of a yearly tenancy, six months,
   - in the case of a tenancy where the period is less than a month, one month, and,
   - in any other case, a period equal to the period of the tenancy.)

   (b) the first anniversary of the start of the first period of the tenancy except in the case of–
   - a statutory periodic tenancy, which arises when a fixed term assured tenancy ends, or
   - an assured tenancy which arose on the death of a tenant under a regulated tenancy,

   (c) if the rent under the tenancy has previously been increased by a notice under section 13 or a determination under section 14 of the Housing Act 1988, the first anniversary of the date on which the increased rent took effect.

3. The existing rent is   £ _____ per _____

   eg. week, month, year

   This includes/excludes* rates

4. The proposed new rent will be   £ _____ per _____

   eg. week, month, year

   This includes/excludes* rates

   *Cross out whichever does not apply.

- If you agree with the new rent proposed do nothing. If you do not agree and you are unable to reach agreement with your landlord or do not want to discuss it directly with him, you may refer the notice to your local rent assessment committee before the beginning of the new period given in paragraph 2. The committee will consider your application and will decide whether the proposed new rent is appropriate.

- You will need a special form to refer the notice to a rent assessment committee.

To be signed by the landlord or his agent (someone acting for him). If there are joint landlords each landlord or his agent must sign unless one signs on behalf of the rest with their agreement.

Signed

Name(s) of
landlord(s)

Address of
landlord(s)

Tel:

If signed by agent, name and address of agent

Tel: Date: 19

FORM No. 6

Housing Act 1988 section 13(4)

Application Referring A Notice Proposing A New Rent Under An Assured Periodic Tenancy or Agricultural Occupancy to a Rent Assessment Committee

- Please write clearly in black ink.
- Please tick boxes where appropriate.
- When you have filled the form in please send it to the appropriate rent assessment panel.

- You should use this form when your landlord has served notice on you proposing a new rent under an assured periodic tenancy.
- You will need to attach a copy of that notice to this form.
- This form may also be used to refer a notice proposing a new rent or licence fee for an assured agricultural occupancy. In such a case references to "landlord"/ "tenant" can be read as references to "licensor"/"licensee" etc.

1. Address of premises

2. Name(s) of landlord(s)

   Address of landlord(s)

3. Details of premises.
   - (a) What type of property is it, eg house, flat or room(s)?
   - (b) If it is a flat or room(s) say what floor(s) it is on.
   - (c) Give the number and type of rooms, eg living room, bathroom.
   - (d) Does the tenancy include any other facilities, eg garden, garage or other separate building or land?   Yes ☐   No ☐
   - (e) If Yes, please give details.
   - (f) Do you share any accommodation?
     - (i) with the landlord?   Yes ☐   No ☐
     - (ii) with another tenant or tenants?   Yes ☐   No ☐
   - (g) If Yes to either of the above, please give details.

4. What is the current rateable value of the premises?

£

5. (a) When did the present tenancy begin?

19

(b) When does the present tenancy end?

19

6. (a) Did you pay a premium?   Yes ☐   No ☐

(b) If Yes, please give details.

7. Services

(a) Are any services provided under the tenancy (eg cleaning, lighting, heating, hot water or gardening)?   Yes ☐   No ☐

(b) If Yes please give details.

(c) Is a separate charge made for services, maintenance, repairs, landlord's costs of management or any other item?   Yes ☐   No ☐

(d) What charge is payable?

£

(e) Does the charge vary according to the relevant costs?   Yes ☐   No ☐

(f) If Yes, please give details.

8. (a) Is any furniture provided under the tenancy?   Yes ☐   No ☐

(b) If Yes, please give details
(*continue on a separate sheet if necessary*).

9. Improvements

(a) Have you, or any former tenant(s) carried out improvements or replaced fixtures, fittings or furniture for which you or they were not responsible under the terms of the tenancy?   Yes ☐   No ☐

(b) If Yes, please give details
(*continue on a separate sheet if necessary*).

10. What repairs are the responsibility of

   (a)   the landlord?

   (b)   the tenant?
         (*continue on a separate sheet if necessary*).

11. (a)   Give details of the other terms of the ten-
          ancy, eg whether the tenancy is assignable
          and whether a premium may be charged on
          an assignment
          (*continue on a separate sheet if necessary*).

   (b)   Please attach the tenancy agreement, or a
         copy (with a note of any variations), if you
         have one. It will be returned to you as
         quickly as possible.

12. Do you have an assured agricultural occupancy?   Yes ☐   No ☐

13. I/We* attach a copy of the notice proposing a new rent under the assured periodic tenancy
    and I/we* apply for it to be considered by a rent assessment committee.

*To be signed by the tenant or his agent (someone acting for him). If there are joint tenants, each
tenant or his agent must sign, unless one signs on behalf of the rest with their agreement.*

Signed

*Name of
tenant(s)*

*Address of
tenant(s)*

Tel:

If signed by agent, name and address of agent

Tel: *Date:*
                                                              19

*Cross out whichever does not apply.

FORM No. 7

Housing Act 1988 section 20

Notice of an Assured Shorthold Tenancy

- Please write clearly in black ink.
- If there is any thing you do not understand you should get advice from a solicitor or a Citizens' Advice Bureau. before you agree to the tenancy.

- The landlord must give this notice to the tenant before an assured shorthold tenancy is granted. It does not commit the tenant to take the tenancy.
- **This document is important. keep it in a safe place.**

To: [ ]

Name of proposed tenant. If a joint tenancy is being offered enter the names of the joint tenants.

1. *You are proposing to take a tenancy of the dwelling known as:*

[ ]

from [ ] /19 *to* [ ] /19   *The tenancy must be for a term certain of at least six months.*

    day   month   year   day   month   year

2. This notice is to tell you that your tenancy is to be an assured shorthold tenancy. Provided you keep to the terms of the tenancy. you are entitled to remain in the dwelling for at least the first six months of the fixed period agreed at the start of the tenancy. At the end of this period. depending on the terms of the tenancy. the landlord may have the right to repossession if he wants.

3. The rent for this tenancy is the rent we have agreed. However. you have the right to apply to a rent assessment committee for a determination of the rent which the committee considers might reasonably be obtained under the tenancy. If the committee considers (i) that there is a sufficient number of similar properties in the locality let on assured tenancies and that (ii) the rent we have agreed is significantly higher than the rent which might reasonably be obtained having regard to the level of rents for other assured tenancies in the locality. it will determine a rent for the tenancy. That rent will be the legal maximum you can be required to pay from the date the committee directs.

4. This notice was served on you on [19]

To be signed by the landlord or his agent (someone acting for him). If there are joint landlords each must sign. unless one signs on behalf of the rest with their agreement.

Signed [ ]

Name(s) of landlord(s) [ ]

Address of landlord(s) [ ]

Tel: [ ]

If signed by agent, name and address of agent

Tel: ☐ Date: ☐ 19

Special note for existing tenants

- Generally if you already have a protected or statutory tenancy and you give it up to take a new tenancy in the same or other accommodation owned by the same landlord, that tenancy cannot be an assured tenancy. It can still be a protected tenancy.

- But if you currently occupy a dwelling which was let to you as a protected shorthold tenant, special rules apply.

- If you have an assured tenancy which is not a shorthold under the Housing Act 1988, you cannot be offered an assured shorthold tenancy of the same or other accommodation by the same landlord.

FORM No. 8

Housing Act 1988 section 22(1)

Application to a Rent Assessment Committee for a Determination of a Rent Under an Assured Shorthold Tenancy

- Please write clearly in black ink.

- Please tick boxes where appropriate.

- A tenant with a fixed term assured short-hold tenancy may use this form to apply to the local rent assessment committee, during the fixed term, to have the rent reduced. This form cannot be used in the cases specified at the end of this form.

- The form may also be used to apply to have the rent reduced for a fixed term assured shorthold tenancy which is an assured agricultural occupancy. In such a case. references to "landlord"/"tenant" can be read as references to "licensor", "licensee" etc.

- When you have filled the form in please send it to the appropriate rent assessment panel.

1. Address of premises

2. Name(s) of landlord(s)

   Address of landlord(s)

3. Details of premises.
   (a) What type of property is it. eg house, flat or room(s)?

   (b) If it is a flat or room(s) say what floor(s) it is on.

   (c) Give the number and type of rooms, eg living room, bathroom etc.

   (d) Does the tenancy include any other facilities, eg garden, garage or other separate building or land?

   Yes ☐   No ☐

   (e) If Yes, please give details.

   (f) Do you share any accommodation?
   (i) with the landlord?   Yes ☐   No ☐
   (ii) with another tenant or tenants?   Yes ☐   No ☐

   (g) If Yes to either of the above. please give details.

4. What is the current rateable value of the premises?

   £

5.   (a)   When did the present tenancy begin?

                                                                   19

    (b)   When does the present tenancy end?

6.   (a)   Please confirm by ticking box that you received a notice saying that the tenancy ☐
was to be an assured shorthold tenancy before the agreement was entered into.

    (b)   Attach a copy of the notice if available.
It will be returned without delay.

7.   (a)   Did you pay a premium?   Yes ☐   No ☐

    (b)   If Yes, please give details.

8. Services

    (a)   Are any services provided under the tenancy   Yes ☐   No ☐
(eg cleaning, lighting, heating, hot water or
gardening)?

    (b)   If Yes, please give details.

    (c)   Is a separate charge made for services,   Yes ☐   No ☐
maintenance, repairs, landlord's costs of
management or any other item?

    (d)   What charge is payable?   £

    (e)   Does the charge vary according to the   Yes ☐   No ☐
relevant costs?

    (f)   If Yes, please give details.

9.   (a)   Is any furniture provided under the tenancy?   Yes ☐   No ☐

    (b)   If Yes, please give details
(*continue on a separate sheet if necessary*).

10. What repairs are the responsibility of

    (a)   the landlord?

    (b)   the tenant?
(*continue on a separate sheet if necessary*).

11. (a)   Give details of the other terms of the tenancy. eg whether the tenancy is assignable.
and whether a premium may be charged on
an assignment
(*continue on a separate sheet if necessary*).

```
┌─────────────────────────┐
│                         │
├─────────────────────────┤
│                         │
├─────────────────────────┤
│                         │
├─────────────────────────┤
│                         │
└─────────────────────────┘
```

(b)   Please attach the tenancy agreement or a copy (with a note of any variations) if you
have one. It will be returned to you without delay.

12. The existing rent is

```
┌─────────────────────────┐
│ £               per     │
└─────────────────────────┘
```
eg. week, month, year

This includes/excludes*   rates of

```
┌─────────────────────────┐
│ £               per     │
└─────────────────────────┘
```

13 I/We* apply to the rent assessment committee to determine a rent for the above mentioned
premises.

*To be signed by the tenant or his agent (someone acting for him). If there are joint tenants each
tenant or his agent must sign, unless one signs on behalf of the rest with their agreement.*

Signed

Name(s) of
tenant(s)

Address
of tenant(s)

Tel:

If signed by agent, name and address of agent

Tel: Date: 19

- An application cannot be made if–
  (a)   the rent payable under the tenancy is a rent previously determined by a rent assessment
  committee: or
  (b)   the tenancy is an assured shorthold tenancy that came into being on the ending of a
  tenancy which had been an assured shorthold of the same, or substantially the same,
  property and the landlord and tenant under each tenancy were the same at that time.

- The rent assessment committee cannot make a determination unless it considers–
  (a)   that there is a sufficient number of similar dwelling-houses in the locality let on assured
  tenancies (whether shorthold or not); and
  (b)   that the rent payable under the shorthold tenancy in question is significantly higher
  than the rent which the landlord might reasonably be expected to get in comparison
  with other rents under the assured tenancies mentioned in (a) above.

Cross out whichever does not apply.

FORM No. 9

Housing Act 1988 section 41(2)

Notice by Rent Assessment Committee
Requiring Further Information

To: _____   *Landlord(s)/tenant(s)**

of: _____   *Address of premises*

1. An application has been made to the rent assessment committee for consideration of–
   * the terms of a statutory periodic assured tenancy
   * an increase in rent under an assured periodic tenancy
   * the rent under an assured shorthold tenancy
   * an increase in rent under an assured agricultural occupancy

   of the above property. The committee needs more information from you, to consider the application.

2. The information needed is

   Please send it to

   no later than   19

3. If you fail to comply with this notice without reasonable cause you will be committing a criminal offence and may be liable to a fine.

Signed _____   Date _____ 19

for the rent assessment committee

*Cross out whichever does not apply.

EXPLANATORY NOTE

(This note is not part of the Regulations)

These Regulations prescribe the forms to be used for the purposes of various provisions of Part 1 of the Housing Act 1988 relating to assured tenancies and assured agricultural occupancies.

STATUTORY INSTRUMENTS

1988 No. 2236

LANDLORD AND TENANT, ENGLAND AND WALES

The Assured and Protected Tenancies (Lettings to Students) Regulations 1988

Made	21st December 1988
Laid before Parliament	22nd December 1988
Coming into force	15th January 1989

In exercise of the powers conferred on the Secretary of State by section 8 of the Rent Act 1977(**a**) and paragraph 8 of Schedule 1 to the Housing Act 1988(**b**), the Secretary of State for Education and Science, as respects England, and the Secretary of State for Wales, as respects Wales, hereby make the following Regulations:

1. These Regulations may be cited as the Assured and Protected Tenancies (Lettings to Students) Regulations 1988 and shall come into force on 15th January 1989.

2. In these Regulations –

"assisted" has the same meaning as in section 114(2)(b) of the Education Act 1944(**c**);
"further education" means –

> (a) full-time and part-time education for persons over compulsory school age (including vocational, social, physical and recreational training); and
> (b) organised leisure-time occupation provided in connection with the provision of such education;

but does not include higher education;

"higher education" means education provided by means of a course of any description mentioned in Schedule 6 to the Education Reform Act 1988(**d**);
"publicly funded" shall mean that the relevant institution is –

> (a) provided or assisted by a local education authority;
> (b) in receipt of grant under regulations made under section 100(1)(b) of the Education Act 1944(**e**); or
> (c) within the PCFC funding sector by virtue of section 132 of the Education Reform Act 1988; and

"the relevant enactments" means section 8 of the Rent Act 1977 and paragraph 8 of Schedule 1 to the Housing Act 1988 (lettings to students).

3. The following institutions are hereby specified as educational insitutions for the purposes of the relevant enactments, that is to say –

(**a**) 1977 c.42.
(**b**) 1988 c.50.
(**c**) 1944 c.31; section 114(2)(b) is prospectively repealed in part by Schedule 13 to the Education Reform Act 1988 (c.40).
(**d**) 1988 c.40.
(**e**) 1944 c.31; section 100(1)(b) was amended by section 213(3) of the Education Reform Act 1988.

(a) any university or university college and any constituent college, school or hall or other institution of a university;

(b) any other institution which provides further education or higher education or both and which is publicly funded;

(c) the David Game Tutorial College, London.

4. The following bodies of persons (whether unincorporated or bodies corporate) are hereby specified as bodies for the purposes of the relevant enactments, that is to say –

(a) the governing body of any educational institution specified in Regulation 3 above;

(b) the body, other than a local education authority, providing any such educational institution, and

(c) a body listed in the Schedule to these Regulations.

5. The Protected Tenancies (Exceptions) Regulations 1986**(a)** and the Protected Tenancies (Exceptions) (Amendment) Regulations 1988**(b)** are hereby revoked.

SCHEDULE
SPECIFIED BODIES UNDER REGULATION 4(C)

AFSIL Limited
Birmingham Friendship Housing Association
Bishop Creighton House, London
Carrs Lane Church Centre, Birmingham
Ducane Housing Association Limited
The City University Students' Union
Hamtun Housing Association Limited, Southampton
Hull Students Welfare Association
International Students Housing Society, Woolwich
International Students Trust, London
Leicester University Students Union
London House for Overseas Graduates, London
Oxford Overseas Student Housing Association Limited
Oxford Polytechnic Housing Association Limited
St Thomas More Housing Society Limited, Oxford
Student Homes Limited, London
The University of Sussex Catholic Chaplaincy Association
Victoria League for Commonwealth Friendship, London
Wandsworth Students Housing Association Limited
York Housing Association Limited

(a) S.I. 1986/541.
(b) S.I. 1988/1683.

EXPLANATORY NOTE

(This note is not part of the Regulations)

Section 8 of the Rent Act 1977 and paragraph 8 of Schedule 1 to the Housing Act 1988 excepts from the definition of "protected tenancy" and "assured tenancy" in section 1 of the respective Acts a tenancy granted to a student, or prospective student, at an educational institution specified for the purposes of the said section 8 or paragraph 8 by regulations if the tenancy is granted by such an institution or by a body so specified.

These Regulations consolidate the Regulations specifying insitutions and bodies for the purposes of section 8 and specifies the same and certain other institutions and bodies for the purposes of the said paragraph 8.

Table of Cases

Table of Statutes

Index

alienation, 84
  assured periodic tenancies, 39–40
  fixed term tenancies, 39
appeals, 74
associated companies, 88
assured shorthold tenancies
  assured tenancy, turning into, 45
  BES, in relation to, 82
  definition of, 43–4
  features of, 1–2
  fixed term, recovery of
    possession of, 45
  periodic, recovery of possession
    of, 45–6
  prevention of, 51
assured tenancies
  BES, in relation to, 79–80, 82
  cessation of, 11
  conversion of, 53–4
  definition, 8
  exceptions to, 53
  features of, 1, 36
  features of, under HA 1980, 4–5
  regulation of, 89
  tenancy, meaning of, 8–9
  tenancy, which cannot be, 12–17
  use of, under HA, 1980, 7

business expansion schemes (BES)
  capital gains tax advantages of,
    82
  income tax advantages of, 81
  investors, relief for, 80
  investors, rights of, 80–81
  limitations of, 82
  qualifying activities, companies,
    79–80
  qualifying activities, individuals,
    80

business tenancies, 13

county court jurisdiction, 42, 65–6
crown tenancies, 16

dwelling house
  illegal or immoral usage, 29
  includes other land, 9–10
  meaning of, 9–10, 11
  separate nature of, 9–10, 36
  valuation of, in relation to BES,
    82

eviction
  damages for, 64–5
  defences and mitigation, 63–4
  liability for, 62–3
  necessary for court order, 66
  offer of reinstatement, 64
  safeguards against, 66–8
  tortious nature, 62–3
  unlawful, 60

fair rent, 50, 52, 69, 72, 74, 77, 110
  fixing of, 52, 76–7
family, 56–7

harassment
  damages for, 62
  defence against, 61
  offences of, 61–2
  penalties for, 62
  unlawful, 60
Housing Act 1988
  generally, 1–3
  text of, 95–147
housing association lettings and
  licenses, 52
housing benefit, 77